LEADERSHIP AND DIVERSITY

Leadership and Diversity

Challenging Theory and Practice in Education

Jacky Lumby
with
Marianne Coleman

SAGE Publications
Los Angeles • London • New Delhi • Singapore

SAGE Publications Ltd
1 Oliver's Yard
55 City Road
London EC1Y 1SP

SAGE Publications Inc
2455 Teller Road
Thousand Oaks, California 91320

SAGE Publications India Pvt Ltd
B 1/I 1 Mohan Cooperative Industrial Area
Mathura Road, Post Bag 7
New Delhi 110 044

SAGE Publications Asia-Pacific Pte Ltd
33 Pekin Street #02-01
Far East Square
Singapore 048763

British Library Cataloguing in Publication data

A catalogue record for this book is available from the
British Library

ISBN 978-1-4129-2182-4
ISBN 978-1-4129-2183-1 (pbk)

Library of Congress Control Number: 2006934506

Typeset by Dorwyn, Wells, Somerset
Printed in Great Britain by Athenaeum Press, Gateshead,
Tyne & Wear
Printed on paper from sustainable resources

Contents

Notes on the authors

Jacky Lumby

Jacky Lumby is Professor of Education at the University of Southampton. She has taught and led in a range of educational settings, including secondary schools, community and further education. She has researched and published widely on leadership and management in schools and colleges in the UK and internationally.

Marianne Coleman

Marianne Coleman is a Reader in Educational Leadership and Management at the Institute of Education, University of London. Her career has been in education, mainly teaching in schools and universities. Her research is in the area of educational leadership and management, with a particular interest in women in educational leadership.

Series Editor's Foreword

This series of books recognises that leadership in education in the twenty-first century has an increasingly moral dimension. As education is seen more and more as being central to the transformation of society, its leaders have an onerous responsibility in their roles and within their organisations to address issues that affect the development of greater social justice. Whilst education is, fortunately, no longer seen as the panacea for all of a nation's problems, it remains central to the progress of most countries, both developed and developing, in their attempts to ensure their economic and social futures.

For those in education, leadership for social justice involves confronting major issues, such as those of equity, diversity and inclusion, in stimulating the changes needed for the embedding of social justice. What educational leaders need to reflect on, what actions they need to take, how they should be developed and how education should link and work with other disciplines and services are all important components in the social justice agenda.

This book, by Jacky Lumby and Marianne Coleman, both of whom are noted and experienced writers and researchers, focuses on leadership for diversity and offers a major challenge for those researching and practising in this field. The authors confront the complexities inherent in the term 'diversity' and, through a detailed consideration of current research and literature, show the inadequacy of how leadership in education has conceptualised it to date.

Drawing on socio-biological and psychological theory, as well as educational, they explore these complexities and show how easy it is for organisations, often unintentionally, to obstruct the ways of grasping the real considerations involved in acknowledging 'equity in difference'. Believing that diversity is about people's strengths and their differences, they argue that the context is now right for concern about, for example, equal opportunities and feminism, to be encompassed within the wider notion of diversity.

As the concepts and the problems are complex, so the possible solutions are equally so, and the authors readily concede that no simple answers exist. However, the work of this book is grounded in a belief that there is cause for optimism, and the authors offer the reader ideas for action which may help to promote diversity by and for educational leaders. This book breaks new ground and will offer profound challenges for all those involved in any capacity in the field of educational leadership. Leaders who are mindful of the issues raised in this book and who are committed to action for change will find the book an invaluable resource to help them in their quest to embed and institutionalise the way in which difference is valued.

David Middlewood
Series Editor

Preface

This volume is part of a series that aims to contribute to social justice through the transformation of education. It focuses on a key aspect of leadership in education in our increasingly pluralist communities: diversity. Its premise is that the most significant task of educational leadership is to support the development of learners and staff so that all can live lives they value in dignity.

The book originated in a growing perception that though diversity was becoming ever more present in discussion of educational leadership, the concept remains stubbornly peripheral in the main body of literature and in development programmes for leadership. The intention was to undertake a journey to better understand why this was so. We wished to call on our own research and on a wide body of literature, including that from beyond educational leadership. This we hoped would offer a broad range of knowledge and understanding to enrich our engagement with diversity and leadership. The journey has proved intellectually stimulating and emotionally challenging. Our hope is that something of this is communicated to readers as they share the journey. Ultimately our aim was not just to extend our own capacity and that of leaders, but thereby to effect change. There is, of course, a plethora of evidence that change is needed in society, in public services and in education. Whether it is, for example, national reviews following tragic events fuelled by racism, statistics showing the inequality in pay for men and women, or media reflections of tensions between those of different faiths, or sexual orientations, the volatility of relations between individuals and groups is ubiquitously evident. Education is at the heart of hope for change, for it is in our schools, colleges and universities above all that society has the right to expect a model of social justice to be embedded and to be renewed for each generation.

Our focus is on leaders and leadership, not because we do not believe that diversity raises extremely important issues in relation to all staff and to learners. Rather, we hope that by focusing on leadership we can firstly explore issues in some depth and secondly support current and future leaders to undertake their critical role in working for diversity, equality and inclusion in educational organisations.

The journey undertaken is fraught with difficulties, not least that of language. Even the title of the book is problematic, as the term 'diversity' instantly signifies particular and very different issues to individuals. It is used in multiple ways, but increasingly at the time of writing as synonymous with minority ethnicity. Our intention is to focus on diversity in a much broader sense; that is, the rich plurality of characteristics found in staff within education. This reflects the experience of leaders, who in their work generally relate to individuals, the people who form the staff of their organisation, each of whom may have multiple identities which shift over time. They do not primarily respond to groups such as ethnic minorities or to women or to those with disabilities or of minority sexual orientation.

The structure of the volume reflects the intellectual journey undertaken. We move from exploring the pressures and incentives to consider diversity to the national and organisational action this has evoked and the psychological frameworks for understanding individual response. We focus on the contribution of feminists and those engaged with minority ethnicity to consider whether single or multiple perspectives are helpful. We then move on to formulate aims for educational leaders. Finally, we consider what change might be needed in both the theory and practice of leadership. Chapters 1–3, 6, 7 and 9 were written by Jacky Lumby. Marianne Coleman wrote Chapters 4, 5 and 8. Both of us commented fully on drafts of all chapters.

The book is international in perspective in that it draws on literature from many countries throughout the globe. However, it does not and could not adequately reflect the abundant variation in context, issues and ethical/spiritual stance. For example, we are aware that the premise that equality and inclusion are desirable is not necessarily shared in all societies. We are particularly aware that the degree of discrimination and the detriment which follows is qualitatively different in some parts of the world and we have not been able to encompass such issues as they deserve. The volume largely reflects the orientation of Anglophone countries and we acknowledge this. Very many books are needed to address the full range of relevant issues throughout the world. This one volume makes a contribution but cannot encompass all that it would be desirable to address.

We would like to thank a number of people for their help. Marianne Lagrange at Sage was a supportive commissioning editor. Colleagues at the University of Lincoln and the London Institute of Education have over time taught us much. Alma Harris, Marlene Morrison, Krishan Sood and Daniel Muijs worked on the 'Leading Learning' research project, which provides some of the data used in the volume. David Middlewood and Ann Briggs made helpful comments on a draft of Chapter 6. We also pay tribute to each other, for determination to stick to the task and to work through differences in perspective. The journey has been demanding but exhilarating, and we hope that in response readers will be stimulated to reflection and to action in this most crucial endeavour of education.

Jacky Lumby
Marianne Coleman

1

Introduction: Diversity, leadership and education

I'm tending to be a bit dismissive about this issue to be frank, saying well really all these diversity issues ... I personally don't feel very switched on to the idea of diversity ... I just feel a little bit amused about it.

(Senior leader in education, 2004)

Key terms and definitions

The first section of this introductory chapter is designed to orientate the reader to the broad purpose and thrust of the book. It gives working definitions of key terms and allows the reader a brief glimpse of the ideas that are core to the book, and which are developed in more depth in the rest of the chapter.

The book focuses on leadership and diversity in education. The term diversity is chameleon-like, taking on different meanings for people over time. At the period of writing the term is used variously, but the current prevalent use is as synonymous with minority ethnicity. Our understanding of diversity is much wider, reflecting the reality of leading in education where staff have a large range of characteristics which may matter to themselves and to those with whom they work. The everyday usage is indicated by Wikipedia (2006), which defines diversity as 'the presence in one population of a (wide) variety of cultures, ethnic groups, languages, physical features, socio-economic backgrounds, opinions, religious beliefs, sexuality, gender identity, neurology'. Even this extensive list omits aspects of difference which contribute to the diversity of staff, for example, their educational background or age. Diversity is the range of characteristics which not only result in perceptions of difference between humans, but which can also meet a response in others which may advantage or disadvantage the individual in question. This book considers how educational leaders respond to diversity so defined; how they work both for and with diversity; *for* diversity to increase the range of characteristics of people included in leadership, and *with* diversity to ensure that the leadership of all, whatever their characteristics, is productive to the organisation and satisfying to the individual.

Leadership is a second contested concept. We take it to be the conduct of emo-

1

tions, thought and actions which are designed to influence others in a chosen direction. Leadership is evident when the influence is effective to the extent of being discernible by others (Drucker, 1997; Pitt, 1987; Russell, 2003). All educators are potentially leaders, in that all may create followers by influencing those around them, whether as teacher leaders, heads of department, faculty or service support team, bursars, members of a senior leadership team, principal, vice chancellor. We believe all have a role to play in relation to diversity.

Leaders are, of course, concerned with responding to diversity amongst learners. There is a substantial literature concerning the effects of characteristics in learners such as socio-economic background, gender, ethnicity, disability. There is considerable support for reflection on how to support learners so that, whatever their characteristics, they have equal chances to learn. We acknowledge that such endeavours are central to the purpose of educational leaders but the focus of this book is different. It explores the much less considered aspect of leadership relating to equal chances amongst staff, specifically those who are leaders or who aspire to leadership. Its rationale reflects the fact that while there is considerable research on equity for learners there is relatively little on equity for staff. Equity amongst the leadership of an educational organisation is in any case as vital a part of learners' experience as teaching and learning as it models expectations of equality.

The perspective adopted to examine the interplay of leadership and diversity in education is international, drawing on research, issues and practice from a variety of locations. However, the book does not attempt to examine diversity and leadership globally. The context within each country, region and organisation is so varied and distinctive that it would be beyond the scope of one volume to consider leadership and diversity in the education systems in all parts of the world. We recognise also that there are areas, particularly in developing economies, where a specific characteristic such as gender may raise such complex and intransigent issues as to justify a volume in itself. Consequently, rather than attempting to cover leadership and diversity throughout the globe, we have referred internationally to a range of available research. Each reader, wherever they are located, may adopt a critical stance and challenge or take from the volume what appears to them to be stimulating and relevant to their own specifc context.

All educational organisations are within our scope. Diversity is an issue for schools, further/technical/community colleges, higher education, and district and regional admistrations, such as local educational authorities. However, in condsidering leadership for and with diversity in education there is a difficulty in that relatively little relevant research has been undertaken specifically in educational contexts. Consequently, while our focus remains firmly on education, much of the research on which we have drawn is from the wider public and private sectors. This continues longstanding practice. Educational leadership has always been eclectic in adapting research and practice from a range of discplines and contexts for its own different purposes. Additionally, the boundaries between education and the public and private sectors are weakening in some contexts, with schools particularly drawing closer to other pubic sectors, for example, as children's services merge in the UK. Many educational organisations, particularly colleges and universities, consider themselves to be businesses. Drawing on a wider generic literature and relating it to educational contexts is therefore appropriate.

Having briefly highlighted some of the key definitions, the remainder of the chapter delves more deeply into what we intend and why.

The international context

Internationally diversity has become of increasing interest to corporations, the public sector (including education) and other not-for-profit organisations. Exhortations abound to consider diversity and to act variously to conform to the requirements of national and international legislation, to respond to business pressures and to ethical obligations. Leaders have ready access to codes of practice, training programmes, formulae for action. Despite all this, there is a sense that attitudes have not changed fundamentally and shifts in practice have proved relatively superficial in their effects. Dass and Parker (1999, p. 68) suggest that despite the ubiquitous and essentially similar official public statements of organisations committing to equality of opportunity, there is in fact a range of attitudes evident beneath the rhetoric. 'An increasingly diverse workforce is viewed as opportunity, threat, problem, fad or even non-issue.' The failure of even committed employers to generate equality and the gulf between the rhetoric of 'managing diversity' and employees' lived experience is reported repeatedly in the generic literature, for example from the United States of America (USA), Canada and the United Kingdom (UK) (DiTomaso and Hooijberg, 1996; Gagnon and Cornelius, 2000; Maxwell et al., 2001; Sanglin-Grant and Schneider, 2000). In education numerous commentators paint a similar picture (Cochrane-Smith, 1995; Lumby et al., 2005; Mabokela and Madsen, 2003). Rusch (2004, p. 19) suggests that 'silence, blindness, and fear frequently mediate the discourse about diversity and equity among educators'. It would appear that, rather than significant strides being made in relation to diversity and inclusion, formidable 'forces for sameness' (Walker and Walker, 1998, p. 10) prevail. 'White men still hold the best jobs, make the most money, are preferred for promotions, and have the best prospects for future success' (DiTomaso and Hooijberg, 1996, p. 173).

Within this context, this book is driven by various imperatives. It grows out of the commitment of both authors, who have engaged with issues of diversity in educational leadership over two decades. It reflects not only personal commitment, but also more widely, in our view, the increasing urgency with which issues of diversity demand attention. This view is shared by some but is by no means universal. As long ago as 1994, commentators were concluding, 'the types and degree of diversity in organizations have increased greatly to a point where their effects cannot be ignored' (Maznevski, 1994, p. 2). The quotation from a senior leader in education which opens this chapter is drawn from research undertaken by one of the authors in 2004. The words challenge Maznevski's assertion. It would seem that ten years on, leaders in education can and do ignore diversity. Clearly there is variability in the experience of pressure to consider and react to its effects.

Governments and broader groupings of nations have enacted increasingly complex and wide-ranging legislation. European anti-discrimination policy relates to sex, racial and ethnic origin, religion and belief, disability, age and sexual orientation, both within and beyond the labour market. The Human Rights Act 1998, implemented in October 2000, with the UK to be fully compliant by 2007, also has far-reaching implications. Member countries, including the UK, have embedded the European legislation and directives in national laws. In the UK, longstanding legislation, such as the Disabled Persons Acts 1944, 1958, 1986, the Equal Pay Act 1970 (amended 1983), the Sex Discrimination Act 1975 and 1986, the Race Relations Act 1976, have been strenghtend by the addition of a raft of further acts, regulations and codes, including the Disability Discrimination Act 1995, the Sex Discrimination (Gender Reassignment) Regulations 1999, the Race Relations (Amendment) Act 2000, the Employment Act 2002, the Flexible Working Regulations 2002, the Employment Equality (Religion or Belief) Regulations 2003, the Employment Equality (Sexual Orientation) Regulations 2003. The Sex Discrimination Act 1975 has been held to cover lesbians and gay men. The government published a voluntary Code of Practice on Age Diversity in 1999. Legislation on age and disability discrimination was effected in 2006. There is a duty on organisations to promote equality for disabled and black and minority ethnic people and this is being extended to gender in April 2007.

This is not meant to be an inclusive list, but merely uses the UK as an example to indicate the notable rise in legislation in the UK and elsewhere. It is designed to eradicate discrimination and impel people to offer equal opportunities. The range of characteristics which it is assumed may be subject to discrimination grows ever wider; the mandatory arrangements to ensure paid work is feasible for those with children and/or care responsibilities grows ever more complex. The pressure for employers to consider diversity issues is therefore strong and growing. Legislation is a considerable compulsion to address diversity. This book, however, is not about how to comply with legislation or to avoid litigation. Its focus and value base are quite different.

The values of the book

Our intention is to contribute to increasing social justice. This of course can be variously understood. Hayek (1976) suggests that generally those who use the term do not know what they mean by it and therefore its chief purpose is to provide rather vacuous justification for a wide variety of policies and actions. The book is in part an exploration of how we might understand social justice in relation to diversity more exactly, and what action might follow such understanding. Definitions which include terms such as equality or inclusion immediately demand further definition: providing such definition is a major task of the chapters that follow. At the start of the journey, our intention originates in a perception that social justice is not evident in educational leaders and leadership; that is, unjustified benefits and detriment accrue to individuals and groups by virtue of their characteristics. The book explores the mechanisms of such unfairness and considers the different ways in which reduction of detriment might be achieved. How could fairness be understood? Is it a question of equal chances or equal treatment or equal outcomes, for example, or might it be conceived quite differently? Educational leaders should be enabled to live lives they value, in dignity, while contributing productively to their organisation. An increase in social justice is one development that moves us closer to this goal. The remainder of this book will stimulate further reflection on the goal itself and the means to achieve it.

Simons and Pelled (1999, p. 51) suggest 'Diversity is a tricky business which can help you or hurt you.' Navigating amongst the competing conceptions of who is oppressed or disadvantaged and how, amongst people's differing notions of who has a legitimate right to research, to write and to speak reflecting the concerns of varying groups, is indeed a tricky business. The book runs a number of risks. It may be that by exploring various aspects of diversity we risk embedding further perceptions of 'difference' from a norm, or of alienating those who disagree strongly with our analysis. We risk a backlash from those who will see this book as part of an unwarranted attention given to diversity, by those who, according to Dass and Parker (1999), see diversity as a fad or non-issue. We are likely to provoke strong emotions in readers. The literature repeatedly attests an emotional reaction to diversity issues or even the term diversity, such as denial, anger and rage (Dass and Parker, 1999; Milliken and Martins, 1996; Osler, 1997). As white women, our right to consider issues affecting those from minority ethnic and other groups to which we do not belong may be questioned, and we acknowledge that there is no way that we can fully understand the alternate realities which grow out of experience very different from our own (Bush et al., 2005). The book will therefore reflect various limitations and – the most significant risk of all – may inadvertently result in perpetuating rather than combating inequities (Lorbiecki and Jack, 2000). The latter assert that the idea that diversity issues can be addressed is a fantasy which rests on absurdly naïve apolitical analyses or simplifications of complex political and social phenomena. While we recognise much truth in this, we reject a pessimistic determinism which refuses to act because action is futile.

Failing to act can only serve the interests of the dominant in organisations and society (Reynolds and Trehan, 2003; Rusch, 2004).While the risks outlined above are real, our assumption is that increasing knowledge and deepening reflection may, over time, bring about positive change. We are in agreement with Reynolds and Trehan's (2003, p. 167) belief in 'the importance of difference being deconstructed, understood and confronted'. We wish to contribute to the exposure of the mechanisms of inequity, on the grounds that mere goodwill is insufficient. As many corporations and public sector organisations have found, those with a genuine commitment to responding positively to diversity may still be confounded by the chasm between intended and actual effect. Research reports outline the frequent gulf between how senior managers believe the company acts in relation to diversity and employees' very different perspective (Gagnon and Cornelius, 2000). International companies which believe themselves to be at the forefront of diversity policy and practice are shaken by litigation instigated by employees who consider they have been treated unfairly (Dass and Parker, 1999). In schools and colleges, the same gulf appears between the intention of leaders and the experience of staff (Bush et al., 2005; Lumby et al., 2005). Training on disability or diversity, instead of achieving the intended effect of greater awareness and support, can result in antagonism and resentment (Stone and Colella, 1996). Greater understanding of cause and effect is needed to support effective action.

We believe that education, while it reflects society, may also have a role in leading society. Schools, colleges and universities are not only employers with the responsibility to facilitate ways of working that allow all staff to live in dignity and to work productively; they also thereby act as models to their learners and to their communities. They have a double obligation reflecting their cultural and social centrality. We reject means–ends attitudes to human beings and believe that, in any case, ultimately, paradoxically, such attitudes may not serve the efficiency needs of organisations, though they may appear to do so in the short term. The book rests on the assumption that many in education will value humans for themselves and not just for their usefulness to the organisation, and therefore welcome a stimulus for reflection. A second assumption is that leaders at all levels in education in the model they present are key to addressing diversity, not only in their own organisation but also in their community and thereby, ultimately, in wider society.

The centrality of leadership

As the changes described in the first part of this chapter unfold, the role of leadership in relation to diversity is progressively more under scrutiny in a number of ways. Analyses increasingly stress that diversity is related to inequity because of differences in the distribution of power and resource (Lorbiecki and Jack, 2000). Leaders, while they may not be the only people with power in an organisation, by virtue of their formal role of authority, and potentially through other sources of power which have led to them becoming leaders, have the possibility to disturb power relations in ways that may not be open to others. Their validation of the concerns and emotions of those who may feel disempowered or disadvantaged is of importance to such groups (Dreaschlin et al., 2000; Osler, 2004). Their commitment may buffer those who experience a backlash against initiatives related to diversity and inclusion. Their stance, while it may not be decisive, has the potential to orientate the organisation to means–ends attitudes to human beings or to ethical and community-based values. The position of leaders in relation to diversity is therefore of central concern. Secondly, as organisations change in their nature, with many more diverse and fluid ways of working, it may be that leaders are required to lead in different ways. Maznevski (1994) suggests that the skills and techniques that worked in relatively homogeneous institutions are no longer appropriate or effective in organisations that are more diverse. The act of leadership may need to metamorphose. Thirdly, and most fundamentally, how we conceive leaders and leadership may need to transform. Numerous researchers have uncovered evidence of the degree to which the concept of leadership reflects the predilections of the dominant group (Coleman, 2002; Foti and Miner, 2003; Leonard, 1998; Singh, 2002). If the characteristics that translate to success in leader emergence, leader persistence and a leadership career (Foti and Miner, 2003) continue to relate to the current leadership, then we will continue to get copies of the dominant group and to believe them successful. They will match and reinforce the template of leadership which embeds the preferences of the dominant group. In summary, our interest in leadership in relation to diversity reflects knowledge to date which suggests a need for leadership itself to be reconceived and for leaders to lead differently in a more diverse society.

Aims of the book

Within the value base described, the book sets out to achieve the central aim of stimulating reflection on diversity and its implications for leaders in education, with a view to supporting the development of practice. A number of objectives follow:

1 To explore conceptions of diversity.
2 To explore the tensions and possibilities related to addressing broad conceptions of diversity, that is, encompassing a very wide range of characteristics of 'difference', and the tensions and possibilities related to addressing single strands of diversity, such as gender or ethnicity.
3 To explore the links between diversity and context within the UK and internationally.
4 To re-conceptualise leadership to embrace diversity as central rather than as a peripheral or bolt-on issue.
5 To consider how leaders might work for and with diversity.

The term diversity has been used unproblematically in this chapter, but it is of course highly problematic. One of the first objectives in the book therefore will be to explore the varying ways that the term is conceptualised, and more than this, the social and political dimensions evident in the different kinds of conceptualisations. One of the distinctions that will be explored will be between broad and narrow conceptualisations. Broad conceptualisations admit a very wide range of human characteristics as possibly linked to inequity. Narrower conceptualisations select from such characteristics those which appear to elicit a higher degree of possibility of encountering discrimination, for example gender, ethnicity and disability. Gender and ethnicity have been selected as exemplars in the volume. There is no intention to explore the issues connected to gender and ethnicity in depth, each of which would easily take the entire book. Rather, the objective is to explore what might be gained and what lost through focusing on one characteristic rather than multiple characteristics. The choice of these two characteristics inevitably means that other characteristics which could equally have been considered, such as disability, religion, socio-economic class, sexual orientation, will not be subject to the same review.

As our discussion develops, a central question is how far a focus on a single strand or strands is tenable or helpful in relating to the complexity and uniqueness of each human being. The intention therefore is not to present a comprehensive review of how inequity in relation to specific characteristics can be understood and countered. Rather it is to respond to the day-to-day dilemmas of leaders who work with people who have multiple characteristics and to consider how they might conceptualise leadership and act in response.

The consistent focus throughout is leadership. Consequently, a further objective is to consider the ways in which leadership is conceptualised and the impact this has to diminish, maintain or increase the inclusion or exclusion of people from leadership roles. There is, of course, a substantial body of literature considering this issue from the perspective of gender: some, though much less, considering the issue from the perspective of ethnicity. However, the substantive body of literature on 'leadership' remains largely untouched, often apparently oblivious to diversity issues. Exploration of why this is the case and the relationship of leadership theory to exclusion is an objective of the book.

Finally, the book intends not just to support reflection and thereby greater knowledge and understanding of the self, others and organisations. It is also to support action in response. It is not the intention to suggest normative formulae of what should be done. Nor will compliance with the requirements of legislation or the funding bodies for schools, colleges and higher education be assumed to be the motivation for action. Rather, as outlined in the values section above, our assumption is that many people in education believe in the right of all human beings to dignity and to a productive role which allows them to fully utilise their talents. Consequently, the intention is to stimulate reflection on how educators might understand diversity, conceptualise the goals and formulate actions to achieve them. It is about more than working *for* diversity, interpreted as achieving representativeness. It is also about working *with* diversity, that is the potential productive inclusion of all in a diverse leadership. These are ambitious objectives and no doubt our achievement of them may be partial, but we hope to contribute to the body of work reflecting the commitment and efforts of many people over time.

Research base

The book will draw on both literature and our own empirical research. The literature may be characterised as that which directly addresses issues of diversity or particular aspects of diversity such as gender, and literature which, though not focused on diversity, may have relevance for understanding the relationship between leadership and diversity. For example, the research on leader emergence may provide insights into how leadership is conceived and thereby the degree to which it is inclusive or otherwise. Research from the behavioural sciences on group and individual interactions, from political science on power relations, from sociological and historical studies on the interrelation of class and power, may also have considerable relevance. Selected research from the various disciplines suggested above has much to offer the analysis of diversity in leadership. Looking to focus more closely, the body of literature which directly addresses diversity in leadership is limited (Lorbiecki and Jack, 2000). Gender and leadership is the area most fully researched, but even here there is a relatively small body of work as gender issues are generally not prioritised in the education leadership field or more broadly within generic leadership and management (Irby et al., 2002; Sinclair, 2000). The relationship of other characteristics such as ethnicity, disability, religion or sexual orientation to leadership have infrequently been subject to research. As authors, we therefore have to navigate selecting from a large body of literature drawn from specific disciplines, and focusing on the much more limited and somewhat inadequate literature on diversity and educational leadership. We hope the synthesis may offer new insights and stimulus to leaders in education.

We will also be drawing on our own research. This book does not report or draw on a single discrete research project. Rather it will draw on research undertaken by the authors over a number of years reflecting evidence from different phases of education, at different points in time and with different foci. One major project on which it will draw is *Leading Learning*, undertaken in 2003–2004. The project, commissioned by the Learning and Skills Research Centre, investigated aspects of leadership and its development in the Learning and Skills Sector in the UK. It also investigated diversity as a key element of leadership. Ten cases were constructed in different kinds of organisation in the sector; organisations were of various sizes, in different locations in England, and included further, sixth form and specialist-designated colleges, adult and community services and workplace learning providers. A rich range of qualitative and quantative data was collected from focus group and individual interviews and from questionnaire surveys of all staff in each organisation. Staff expressed their views on what form or forms of leadership were prevalent within their organisation, how diversity is understood, the degree of importance attached to the achievement of a diverse leadership and how the latter might be achieved. The methodology is detailed in Lumby et al. (2005).

The book will also draw on research on gender and leadership carried out over a period of ten years and latterly funded by the National College for School Leadership (NCSL). This research has focused on the relationship between gender and leadership particularly in relation to women and men head teachers in England. It has centred round questions of access to leadership in education and the ways in which gender impacts on the perceived experience of head teachers (Coleman, 1996a, 1996b, 2000, 2002, 2005a). The research has been conducted through interviews and major surveys of women and men head teachers and has recently impacted on the work of the NCSL in the development of their programmes. Focus groups, individual interviews and survey research with middle managers relating to gender and ethnicity provide further data and insights (Coleman, 2004, 2005a).

Structure of the book

In summary then, the book considers the pressures to consider and respond to diversity which result from the environment within which educational leaders work. It explores from a number of perspectives in different cultures and contexts the understanding of diversity in a pluralist society and how different conceptions might lead to action in theorising leadership, preparing leaders and the enactment of leadership in education.

Following this introductory chapter, the second chapter considers the developing context. There is variability in the pressure to take account of diversity and in the range of actions which have evolved in response. Business, legislative and ethical pressures to work towards greater equality are explored, comparing the generic context with that in education. The chapter reviews the globally rising level of awareness of diversity in society and specifically in the workforce. It suggests that workplaces now function in qualitatively different ways to previously, for example in more fluid employment contracts and less certain boundaries between the organisation and the community. The implications for equality are considered in the new ordering of employees. It may be that the twenty-first century organisation is even less likely to offer equality than that of the previous century. The chapter also reviews the response to context: the approaches which have been utilised with the intention to increase equality or eradicate inequalities. It examines the shifting terminology, from equal opportunities, to diversity and inclusion, to capabilities approaches, considering policy and action in a number of countries. It explores how far each of the changes in discourse reflect different conceptualisations of the issues raised by diversity in leadership and the different assumptions about the resulting goals and actions to address them.

Chapter 2 is therefore concerned with the big picture, global trends and policy approaches. It concludes that analysis at this level will lead to only partial understanding and reform. Chapter 3 adds a different perspective, that of the psychology of communication and relationships. While there has been relatively little research within education about the experience of being an 'outsider' in leadership, other than that related to gender, research in other public sectors such as health services and within the private sector has revealed something of what causes the experience of being perceived or perceiving oneself as an outsider. Diversity is often seen in some sense as a problem in itself. The third chapter refutes this and suggests that, in part, the root of inequality is the way diversity is conceived and the fearful attitudes towards diversity which are profoundly embedded in human relations. Such anxiety underlies the creation of in-groups, out-groups and the outsider experience. The chapter explores how the idea of 'other' is created at the individual and group level and considers the place of individual strategies for change at the personal level.

Internationally, the teaching profession tends to be numerically dominated by women, but in most countries, women do not occupy a commensurate proportion of senior leadership and management roles. The fourth chapter addresses issues of gender equity in accessing leadership roles in a number of countries, and the impact of gender on women and men educational leaders. The frame of gender allows consideration of what may be gained and lost through a focus on a single characteristic of diversity.

Similarly, in the fifth chapter, ethnicity is considered discretely. The student population of schools and colleges internationally, particularly in urban areas, is increasingly ethnically diverse. However, this diversity is not mirrored in the teaching community, where the number of black and minority ethnic educational leaders remains very small. This chapter addresses the current state of knowledge about the experience of being an educational leader from a black or minority ethnic background, taking into account current policy and practice in a number of countries. Different countries' engagement with a range of interventions such as anti-racist policies, targeted training and affirmative action are considered. The central question is whether issues that arise from attitudes and reactions to black and minority ethnic leaders, current and potential, are best addressed with a single focus or through incorporation into a generic view.

Leadership itself comes under the spotlight in Chapter 6, which argues that current theories of leadership in fact embed ever further the hegemonic attitudes and practice which ensure that a diverse leadership, if ever achieved, is likely to face problems in being effective. The chapter considers a number of different theories of leadership, including transformational, distributed, democratic and authentic, and explores how far each takes account of the diversity or potential diversity of leadership. The chapter questions the assumptions embedded in some theories that consensus and 'common good' are achievable and the foundation of effective leadership. It proposes that to be inclusive leadership theory must reject false notions of consensus and assume ongoing conflict and disagreement as the bedrock of leadership. The chapter contributes to a development of leadership theory fit for the more diverse context of schools, colleges, universities and their communities.

Chapter 7 draws together the threads of the exploration of previous chapters. It suggests that while we should not abandon what we have learned from focusing specifically on single characteristics such as ethnicity, gender and disability, nor set aside initiatives to address the disadvantage likely to be encountered by particular groups, a more holistic approach is needed, both in terms of encompassing the very many ways in which individuals can be in a position of disadvantage, and to embed diversity within leadership theory and practice, rather than as a parallel and minor adjunct.

The final two chapters focus on what change might be needed to ensure the recruitment of leaders is inclusive and that a diverse leadership is both productive and equally supportive to all members. Chapter 8 reviews initiatives undertaken at operational level to support access to and the practice of leadership by diverse groups. It includes consideration of the role of policy, data collection and use, training and development. Chapter 9 tackles the issue of change at a variety of cognitive and structural levels. While there is much rhetoric and exhortation to view diversity as a positive feature within leadership, research indicates that it can in fact be counter-productive and may lead to less efficient working among leadership groups. At the same time, research also indicates that diversity amongst leaders has the potential of leading to a better performance. This chapter explores how leaders might approach harnessing diversity in leadership as a positive factor and what actions are needed to overcome the difficulties created not by diversity, but by attitudes towards it and by entrenched structures and working practices.

Risks and rewards

Smith (1997) suggests that those who question existing practice and suggest new ideas within leadership and management are often punished by other team members. There is certainly no dearth of scathing comment in the literature targeted at those who adopt a particular stance or suggest particular actions in relation to diversity. Lorbiecki and Jack (2000, p. 29) castigate the adoption of 'the everyone-is-different metaphor'. Others pour scorn on 'diversity management', suggesting it is but the latest in a line of vehicles for making sure diversity is *not* addressed (Sinclair, 2000). Litvin (1997) undermines the very notion of categorising 'difference' into groups such as black and ethnic minorities, as based on inappropriate notions of essentialism derived from the natural sciences. There is no safe ground anywhere in discussing diversity, no agreement on any aspect, not even that diversity is an issue at all, let alone how one should act in response. We have set out our stall in this introductory chapter. We believe, like Milliken and Martins (1996, p. 14) that the 'tendency to drive out diversity is an extremely serious and systematic force'. The appropriate response is to engage critically, reflexively and with humility, recognising that the contribution this book can make is partial, imperfect and limited. Nevertheless, our intention is to make a contribution, to stand on the shoulders of all those who have gone before and to offer some insights of value to those who will be in a position to act as leaders, colleagues, researchers and writers. To our mind, no action is no option.

2

Equality approaches: What's in a name?

Drivers of change

This chapter explores the pressures on leaders to respond to diversity and the way the issues and consequent actions have been conceptualised. The first part of the chapter considers demographic, legislative and ethical pressures. The second part discusses how organisations have responded by conceptualising the issues and actions which follow. The chapter draws largely upon generic literature because there is no equivalent body focused on education or educational leadership. However, the implications for educational leaders are drawn from the consideration of generic contexts.

Changing demographics

The impetus to address issues of inequity in employment could arguably be traced back in history for millennia. The appointment of those favoured because they were of the ruling class or ethnic group or men has provoked a response in a variety of forms over time. However, embedding such an impetus in wide-ranging legislation is relatively recent. Equal pay for men and women was established as a principle by the International Labour Organisation in 1951 and equal treatment in 1958, but it was some years before the states which had endorsed the principles began to enact them through legislation (Vogel-Polsky, 1985). In the latter part of the twentieth and early twenty-first centuries, attention has sharpened as demographic changes have elicited concern about how the response of leaders to increasing diversity would maintain or erode their business position. Workforce mobility is growing as migration increases across the globe. Electronic communication and siting a workforce in one or more countries distant from physical headquarters is challenging organisations to consider the needs not just of employees with disabilities, of different ethnic backgrounds and gender, but in relation to many other dimensions such as culture and religion. The USA was in the forefront in recognizing the implications. In 1987, the *Workforce 2000* report (Johnson and Packer, 1987)

> informed North Americans that by the year 2000 the majority of its workers would be African-Americans, Hispanics, Native Americans, women and other 'minority' groups ... the relegation of white males to 'minority' group status caused organizations in the USA to consider who their future managers might be. (Lorbiecki and Jack, 2000, p. 20)

The statistics continue to exercise US business leaders. In a 2003 speech the Senior Vice President of US United Parcel Service (with a workforce of more than a third of a million) informed his audience that 35 per cent of the workforce and 52 per cent of appointments in his company were from minority groups, well above the nationally predicted 27 per cent (Darden, 2003). Other countries and regions, such as Australia and the European Community, have reported similar retrospective accounts and prognostications of further change:

> Forty per cent of Australians are either themselves migrants or children of migrants and almost one sixth speak a language other than English at home. (Patrickson and Hartman, 2001, p. 199)

The number of women entering the workforce and leadership roles has also steadily increased (Singh, 2002; Weiss, 1999). The possibility that white males may be a minority of entrants to the labour force has particularly focused the mind of employers on the implications of increasing diversity (Dreaschlin et al., 2000; Maxwell et al., 2001). Education has reflected similar concerns. The potential shortage of and increased diversity amongst leaders has heightened awareness of the need to increase representation and ensure the productivity of diverse teams in schools, colleges and universities (Bush et al., 2005; Hartle and Thomas, 2003).

There is, however, something of a dislocation of experience between those living in urban and those living in rural environments, for example in China, in South Africa, in France. While those living in cities and particularly metropolises would generally recognise demographic shifts, those in rural settings may have experienced relatively less change in the profile of their community (Coleman, 2002). There is not a consistent dichotomy, but the pressure of changing demographics may vary considerably from country to country, area to area.

The primary driver in business appears to be the necessity to ensure that an inevitably more heterogeneous workforce would function as productively as the previously more homogeneous one. However, faced with an unavoidable change, some looked to make a virtue of the process. Not only would the workforce be as productive as previously, it might be *more* productive because of its diversity. It is argued that a more diverse workforce, 'a wider talent pool' (Singh, 2002, npn), would improve performance in a number of ways. For example, by bringing a wider range of perspectives to bear, decision making would improve. Marketing would be strengthened by employees having greater awareness of the different life experience of a wider range of consumers (Maznevski, 1994). Heterogeneity, it was hoped, would pay. However, this optimistic, simplistic judgement is increasingly questioned and tempered. Heterogeneity pays, in some contexts and some circumstances. Equally, the opposite may be true, and performance may be undermined by diversity (Milliken and Martins, 1996). The issue is therefore not changing demographics, but 'the inability of work organizations to truly integrate and use a heterogeneous workforce at all levels of the organization' (Mor Barak, 2000).

The greater diversity in populations and the workforce interconnects with changes in organisations and organisational practice, outlined by DiTomaso and Hooijberg (1996, p. 171):

- Increasing permeability of organisational boundaries (i.e. the boundaryless organisation).
- Increasing interconnections among organisations (networks, alliances, partnerships and such).
- Increasing educational and technical specialization among larger segments of employees (the knowledge-based organisation).
- Increasing interdependence in work among all employees (the integrative organization; need for high performance teams).
- Increasing customization of products and services (the post-industrial corporation).
- The externalization of risk, resulting in the 'hollowing' of corporations, through subcontracting, licensing, the use of temporary employees and, in government, through privatization.

Those who work in education in many parts of the world can relate to this depiction of change with ease. Each of DiTomaso and Hooijberg's points can be recognised in schools, colleges and universities. In the UK the increasing federation of organisations and permeability of boundaries between schools and other services for children is rapidly resulting in, if not boundaryless organisations, at least organisations with uncertain boundaries. 'Networks, alliances, partnerships and such' are *de rigueur* and, at least rhetorically, permeate education (Lumby and Morrison, 2006). In the USA, the differentiation and specialisation amongst staff as higher level teaching assistants, learning mentors, learning advisors, assessors, information technology specialists, workshop supervisors, bursars etc. continues in leaps and bounds (Levin, 2001). In the UK, workforce remodelling and the Children Act 2004 have demanded staff work in teams, harnessing the specialist skills and experience of an increasingly varied group. Throughout the world, schools, colleges and universities customise by distinguishing themselves along a number of dimensions; becoming a specialist school, a centre of excellence, by faith, by being research-focused, or teaching-focused. Universities such as INSEAD in France, Harvard in the USA and Cambridge in England market themselves through elitism in contrast with other universities, which stress their relatively open access. Faith schools – Muslim, Jewish, Catholic – create a market based on a particular kind of ethos. International schools create an environment which synthesises elements of Western culture to appeal to a particular market (Pearce, 2003; Roberts, 2003). The use of subcontracting, outsourcing and temporary staff is long established, for example in the UK (Woods and Woods, 2005), in Switzerland (Walther et al., 2005) and in Costa Rica (Monge-Najera et al., 2001). While DiTomaso and Hooijberg (1996) may have had commercial corporations in mind, the changes they outline unmistakably map against educational organisations globally.

DiTomaso and Hooijberg call such changes 'revolutionary' and argue that they 'fundamentally reorient the psychological contract between organizations and their employees' (p. 171). Organisations therefore are responding to a workforce that is more diverse, but also to the much greater degree of fluidity, uncertainty and differentiation between people and subunits internally and between organisations externally. In their view, the resulting increasingly complex structures of difference also equate to structures of inequality, as greater competitiveness between groups and insecurity of tenure will advantage some while disadvantaging others. The tensions resulting from inequities are likely to discomfit and so destabilise organisations. The leader's role then is to renegotiate relations and ways of working so that s/he takes responsibility for the psychological wellbeing of employees and the wellbeing of society. The implication is an imperative for leaders to address not only the need for equity and justice within their own organisation, but more broadly in community and society. DiTomaso and Hooijberg suggest that the alternative is increasing polarisation and tribalism which will be destructive of corporations, organisations and communities. This chapter was begun one week to the day after the bombing in London in July 2005. Never had the need to build a more cohesive and just society seemed more compelling. The role of education is of course particularly crucial.

DiTomaso and Hooijberg's arguments link instrumental concerns, for example about securing an adequate workforce by means of recruiting more diversely, and ethical concerns about justice and fairness. Ethical concerns cannot be decoupled from instrumental issues. A just and stable society, or a harmonious and content workforce, are good for business as much as for abstract notions of right. Various commentators have argued that it is possible and necessary to meet both kinds of concern in addressing diversity, that right *and* good can be achieved (Singh, 2002).

Ethical considerations

A second impetus to consider diversity is ethical considerations. There is of course a large literature considering whether ethics can ever be divorced from self-interest. Certainly, some organisations make an explicit link between ethical behaviour and the bottom line. Mor Barak (2000, p. 345) comments on the emergence of the notion of 'corporate social performance' and the increasing assessment of companies' performance against their social impact internally and externally on the community:

> Although there is an acknowledgement that making a contribution to the firm's social environment is an important corporate duty ... there is also accumulating research documenting the connection between the firm's social and ethical policies and its financial performance. (Mor Barak, 2000, p. 345)

Framed in this way, ethics becomes a weapon in the corporate battery for making profit. However, because ethical behaviour may generate profit, it does not mean that an ethical impetus cannot be grounded in a desire to do right, to act justly. Rather than a single determinist economic perspective, the possibility must be entertained that some leaders may wish to address issues of diversity for ethical reasons, because they are committed to social justice. The unfair treatment of some groups in society and the recognition of different perspectives on the nature and purpose of work are acknowledged as demanding attention by many individuals and organisations (DiTomaso and Hooijberg, 1996; Dreachslin et al., 2000). The belief that 'organizations exist to serve human needs' (Irby et al., 2002, p. 308) rather than vice versa, is an increasingly exhorted stance (Gagnon and Cornelius, 2000). However, research suggests that ethical arguments are less evident as a driver of organisations than concerns about organisational performance (Lorbiecki, 2001). Even those in the public sector and not-for-profit organisations who do not have shareholders to satisfy entertain business concerns about maintaining performance through times of demographic change, though the profit motive may not be so evident. Prasad and Mills (1997, p. 10) argue that:

> Theories of human capital explicitly treat people as economic resources; their skills, qualifications and characteristics are regarded as having potential value for firms who hire them. Human capital theories tend to have enormous ideological appeal in Western capitalistic cultures on account of their overtly instrumental arguments; these eventually hold more sway than normative and value-laden positions.

The degree to which this is true of public sector organisations as well as commercial companies is a matter of judgement. The equal opportunities/diversity policies of both kinds of organisation tend to offer normative statements about the ethics of equality. The motivation for the actions to implement policy will vary from leader to leader, organisation to organisation. However, fear of litigation and a desire to maintain business and financial performance appear to be motivators in all types of organisation and generally to hold more weight than ethical considerations (Lorbiecki, 2001).

Education

So far, the discussion has distinguished only between business and the public sector/not for profit organisations. How far does education reflect the same pattern of concerns? First, education may have moved closer to a private sector culture. Schools, colleges and universities have been criticised for some time for adopting an inappropriate business orientation. The critique of managerialism suggests that ethical considerations have weakened in education, displaced by a business culture with a focus on finance and status (Randle and Brady, 1997; Simkins 2000). Consequently one would expect the same concerns to be at the root of attitudes to diversity. Demographic change has certainly been noted:

> Schools operate in an environment characterised by increasing social and cultural diversity ... The political, social and cultural fabric of society between and within communities, cities and regions and countries, and so schools, is becoming increasingly diverse. The children we teach and the communities involved in our schools come from a blossoming array of socio-economic, racial, ethnic and religious backgrounds. (Walker and Walker, 1998, p. 9)

Similarly, Valverde (2006, p. 1) notes the 'ever increasing global migration of people that calls for different models of assimilation, particularly in schools'. However, one difference is notable. In the statement above it is children and their communities which are described as subject to increasing diversity, rather than staff. 'Multiculturalism' and various allied concepts have provided a focus for attention for decades. Consequently, characteristically, many in education are more focused on the issues raised by actual or potential diversity amongst their learners than their colleagues (Lumby et al., 2005). For example, in analysing the anti-racist discourse in Canada and England and Wales, Bonnett and Carrington (1996) discuss learners, but not staff, as the subject of racism. Henze et al. (2001) explore the concept of racial or ethnic conflict relative to leaders in the USA, but the assumption is again that such conflict is amongst learners or in relations between staff and learners, not amongst the staff themselves.

No research has been undertaken into the comparative understanding of and response to diversity issues in schools, technical/community colleges and higher education. However, a tenable hypothesis is that there will be great variation in the priority given to employee and specifically leader diversity issues, depending on the degree to which demographic change is perceived to be evident in the community or organisation. For those schools, colleges and universities where the community/staff are perceived as increasingly diverse and/or there are staff shortages, the priority will be higher. The proportion of schools, colleges and universities where this is not the case, where the perception is of generally continuing homogeneity, is not known. In such organisations, diversity may appear to be a 'non-issue' (Dass and Parker, 1999, p. 68), in education as much as in business. The comment of one middle manager respondent about the staff in a case study in the UK Learning and Skills Sector illustrates both that pupil diversity is seen as the key driver and that lack of demographic change (interpreted here as ethnicity) amongst the staff is of no concern. In fact, it is considered a strength:

We have no ethnic minorities and so obviously that doesn't come into it. We are all quite similar in our background and upbringing, white middle-class, which can be seen either as a strength or weakness. With the current students it is a strength because we have very few ethnic minority students. (Lumby et al., 2005 p. 20)

Diversity is a non-issue for this education leader. The centrality of demographics as a driver is equally apparent in the thinking of a respondent in a second case in the same study:

[Area in which organisation is located] traditionally has never had any black areas. Even now when there's lots of refugees coming, they don't put black refugees here ... It's not on the agenda – that's my perception ... I don't think diversity by that definition is a problem here. (Lumby, 2006, p. 157)

There is undoubtedly a range of literature emphasising the importance of values in education and specifically the necessity to address diversity in leadership (Begley, 2004; Boscardin and Jacobson, 1996; Gold et al., 2003). This literature is discussed in detail in Chapter 6. Nevertheless, despite such literature, there is insufficient empirical evidence to conclude whether ethical or demographic issues, or any others, are driving educational leaders in the UK or elsewhere to consider diversity issues any more than previously. What is apparent is that the variation amongst educational organisations in their stance to diversity may be just as wide as amongst commercial organisations. It cannot be assumed that ethical issues are any more potent as a motivator in education than elsewhere.

Conceptualising diversity

So far the term diversity has been used unproblematically, yet it is a shorthand phrase concealing highly contested understandings. Simons and Pelled (1999) suggest it is usually connected in people's thinking with ethnicity and gender. Research in the UK Learning and Skills Sector suggested that while leaders understood diversity in many different ways, ethnicity was the most common connotation in people's minds (Lumby et al., 2004). Delving beneath the common, unreflective usage of the term, there lies the belief that people can be categorised into identifiable groups by means of a range of characteristics. Litvin (1997) explores the process of categorisation and suggests that diversity originates in a tradition of essentialism and scientific taxonomy stretching back to Plato:

The emphasis had been on delineating categories of organisms based on observed similarities, on identifying species and sub-species and on constructing organisational hierarchies structuring the relationships among the various species the naturalist observed. (Litvin, 1997, pp. 188)

More recent work concerned with biodiversity and human diversity, fuelled by progress in genetics, has strengthened the impetus to categorise human beings. The embedded assumptions are reflected in the diversity discourse:

> With its adoption of diversity, managerial discourse has unreflectively incorporated essentialist ontological assumptions from the realm of natural science. (Litvin, 1997, p. 188)

However, Litvin challenges whether such assumptions are tenable in the light of increasing certainty in natural science that whatever taxonomy is adopted, the complexity of human beings, biologically, linguistically and culturally, cannot be placed into immutable and easily described groups: 'The categories constructed through the discourse of workforce diversity as natural and obvious are hard pressed to accommodate the complexity of real people' (1997, p. 202). Natural science has attempted divisions of humanity by geographic origin, genetic components and linguistic patterns. All break down in the face of the incorrigible plurality of humanity.

Despite the intractability of categories, leaders persist in referring to them as a given and act upon the assumption of categories. Sometimes the factors by which groups are identified are finite. Lorbiecki and Jack (2000), for example, take diversity to embrace race, culture, ethnicity, age, disability and experience of work. Others avoid a finite categorisation and recognise that the characteristics, singly and in combination, which could disadvantage an individual are infinite and therefore diversity cannot relate to groups but to accommodating all individuals. Singh (2002, p. 36) quotes the British supermarket Tesco: 'Diversity is recognising individuality.'

This distinction can be seen as broad and narrow definitions of the dimensions of difference (Wentling and Palma-Rivas, 2000, p. 36). Broad definitions incorporate a wide range of criteria, including age, disability, religion, sexual orientation, values, ethnic culture, national origin, education, lifestyle, beliefs, physical appearance, social class and economic status (Norton and Fox, 1997). Additionally, diversity can be understood by leaders as a range of attributes, skills and experience involving characteristics such as function, length of service and style of leadership. Narrower definitions focus on those characteristics which are perceived as most likely to disadvantage an individual – ethnicity, gender, disability and age.

A second major strategy of categorisation (besides broad and narrow definitions) is suggested by Simons and Pelled (1999) as observable (such as gender) and non-observable (such as educational background) characteristics. You-Ta et al. (2004, p. 26) describe the same distinction as 'readily detectable or underlying':

> Readily detectable attributes are those that can be determined quickly and with a high degree of consistency by others. Only brief exposure or interaction is required. Readily detectable attributes include age, race, sex, and organizational tenure ... underlying attributes are not so easily or quickly determined by others, such as skills, abilities, knowledge, attitudes and values.

Milliken and Martins (1996) argue that observable differences are more likely to pro-voke discrimination and the greater the degree of observable difference, the more hos-tile the response is likely to be. For example, Stone and Colella suggest that people make aesthetic judgements on the degree to which a physical disability is perceived as attractive or unattractive. The more unattractive the disability is seen to be, the more negative the response. The observable/unobservable categorisation may there-fore be useful in developing understanding about how people respond to diversity.

What emerges is a suggestion that it is not the differences between people that matter, or the way such differences are arranged in patterns through categorisation. What matters is the way others respond to an individual and how that response positions the individual in terms of advantage or disadvantage:

> The attitudes, values, beliefs, and hence, behaviors of individuals are socially constructed within a context of group and intergroup relations and that peo-ple act through social, political, and economic institutions that create, embed, and reproduce the inequality among people which we then call diversity. Diversity is then acted out in the practices of everyday life and interpreted through lenses of moral and ethical reasoning that, when unexamined, legit-imate both unearned privilege and unearned disadvantage. (DiTomaso and Hooijberg, 1996, pp. 164–165)

The key point made by DiTomaso and Hooijberg is that the *response* to differences between individuals and groups leads to unjustified detriment or gain. Conse-quently, narrow definitions are not narrow in the pejorative sense commonly attached to the term. Rather, they are concerned to distinguish 'differences that matter and those that do not, depending on whether they reinforce inequality (Reynolds and Trehan, 2003, p. 167).

Litvin (1997) concludes that the discourse of categorisation of people, that they belong to this group or that, is not the scientific endeavour it appears on the sur-face. Rather it is a distraction from the fact that the categories are mirages, phan-tasms that constantly shift reflecting the power play of everyday interactions:

> The particular differences individuals perceived among one another (as opposed to other, unperceived differences), together with the meanings of those per-ceived differences, are continually constructed through ongoing processes. There are no essential, innate and immutable characteristics of race, age, gender, disability or other demographic categories. Instead there are history, context, process, interactivity, power relations and change. (Litvin, 1997, pp. 206–7)

The purpose of identifying difference and then categorising it into a discernible shape is to support the 'legitimacy of dominating those who have been constructed as in some way inferior' (Reynolds and Trehan, 2003, p. 174). The hidden aspect of concepts of diversity is that people are not only perceived as 'different'; some of them are seen as lesser than others.

The developing discourse

How then have organisations responded, driven by demographic and ethical pressures within this highly political and contested conceptual field? Analysing the discourse is a challenging task. Terms are sometimes used interchangeably, as synonymous, and at other times as having very different meanings. The most prevalent concepts, 'equal opportunities', 'diversity' and 'capabilities', weave their way in and out of the discourse of individual leaders and organisations over time, metamorphosing and also, chameleon-like, camouflaging the same actions in differing terms, or differing stances in the same term.

Equal opportunities

The earliest response was equal opportunities (EO), which emerged as a generic description of an aim, legislation and action undertaken to achieve the aim in the 1960s and 1970s. Maxwell et al. (2001) argue that it was driven by external pressures such as legislation and notions of social justice, and was focused on treating people equally. It was operational in nature, primarily the responsibility of the human resource or personnel staff. It was focused on three groups – women, black and minority ethnic people (BME), and those with disabilities. Its policies and action were shaped by advice from national organisations established to advise on eliminating discrimination against the three groups (Liff and Wacjman, 1996). Equal outcomes were not required by law, but the emphasis on achieving representation of the three groups in education/training and employment at all levels was a strong pressure to see the goal as equal outcomes. The emphasis was on treating all the same by focusing in recruitment and selection only on the essential characteristics required by a job or education/training opportunity and not any other irrelevant factors such as gender or ethnicity. Pay was to be equal. However, in fact, as equal opportunities developed, people were treated differently to a degree. Positive action training for women and black groups, for example, and leave arrangements for parents, recognised the need for some differences in treatment if equal outcomes were to be achieved. Peters (1996) argues that European law grew beyond mere 'equal treatment' to assume that if equality was to be actually achieved rather than merely intended, then action would be needed to rectify the disadvantages under which women, for example, struggled. As a result, differing interpretations of equality, both in law and in public perceptions, have led to decisions to allow and also to disallow positive action, that is action related to one group only to rectify disadvantage, rather than treating all strictly the same.

Diversity

Diversity, or diversity management, tackled achieving equality in an arguably different way. Maxwell et al. (2001) distinguish diversity from equal opportunities in a number of ways. They suggest:

- While the pressures creating equal opportunities initiatives were external, internal business pressures are the driver of diversity measures.
- Diversity is the responsibility of all employees, not primarily human resources.
- It is focused not just on specified groups, but on all individuals in the organisation.
- Difference is to be celebrated and utilised to enhance individuals and the organisation, allowing all to achieve their potential.
- The culture of the organisation is the key focus for change.

Those who are perceived as different from a white, male, middle class norm are not to be obliged to compete on the terms of those in power, to adapt and to become clones. 'It is the mainstream which is expected to adapt, rather than the diverse individuals required to conform' (Wilson and Iles, 1999, p. 36). Singh (2002, p. 28) describes diversity as a 'mosaic pattern of equality through difference'.

While Maxwell et al. confidently distinguish between the two approaches; some of the distinctions could be challenged: for example, the polarity between external pressure driving EO and internal pressures driving diversity. Demographic concern about the rising proportion of women taking jobs from the 1950s onwards led to business concerns that this potential source of talent and growing sector of the workforce must be effectively utilised. This seems parallel to the later business concerns driving diversity measures. Similarly, while human resource staff may have led the process of change, all staff were expected to eradicate discrimination in their practice and that of those they led. Considered more carefully some of the distinctions between the two approaches begin to blur.

A number of positions are discernible. Some are convinced that equal opportunities and diversity are different in the underlying paradigm and the actions which follow. Table 2.1 is an example of confident differentiation between the two.

The distinctions Wilson and Iles (1999) make are similar to those made by Maxwell et al. (2001). While one might question the certainty with which they describe a clearly defined division, an underlying apparent difference in paradigm emerges. In EO, women, BME and people with disabilities were to be aided to compete with the dominant group. They were perceived as lacking one or more characteristics such as confidence, experience, physical abilities, capacity to undertake a career uninterrupted by childrearing, all of which had to be compensated before they could compete successfully on equal terms with white able-bodied men.

Success was to be measured by numeric calculation of representation. Diversity, by contrast, did not start from a deficit model, but an assumption that the differences between people were to be celebrated and integrated, not in the sense of all becoming the same, but all working together harmoniously, making positive use of different life experience, perceptions, attributes and skills. A further significant difference is that while EO initially focused on three groups in society, diversity acknowledged that there were many other characteristics that might disadvantage an individual. Religion, social class, sexuality, educational background and many other characteristics are potentially a dimension of 'difference' and therefore possibly unequal treatment. Positive action may not be required because the differences between people are not a deficit but an advantage. A second concept of inclusion was added to diversity to indicate more explicitly that organisations were not just to encourage the appointment or promotion of both men and women with a wide range of backgrounds and cultures, but that the organisational culture must accommodate and support all. 'Diversity and inclusion' has consequently become something of a mantra, indicating an approach to addressing equity issues which aims at more than just representation. In summary, 'The EO paradigm is trying to right a wrong for identified groups, whereas the MD paradigm is trying to get it right for everyone' (Wilson and Iles, 1999, p. 37). The relation to narrow and broad conceptualisations of difference are clear.

Table 2.1 Differentiating equal opportunities and managing diversity paradigms

Equal Opportunities – the old paradigm	Managing diversity – the new paradigm
Externally driven	Internally driven
Rests on moral and legal arguments	Rests on business case
Perceives EO as a cost	Perceives MD as investment
Operational	Strategic
Concerned with progress	Concerned with outcomes
Rational organisation model	Internalised by managers and employees
Externally imposed on managers	Systematic understanding
	Appreciation of organisational culture
Difference perceived as other/problematical	Difference perceived as asset/richness
Deficit model	Model of plenty
Ethnocentric, heterosexist	Celebrates difference
Assimilation advocated	Mainstream adaptation advocated
Discrimination focus	Development focus
Harassment seen as individual issue	Harassment seen as organisational climate issue
Group focused	Individual focused
Group initiatives	Individual initiatives
Family-friendly policies	Individual development
	Employee friendly policies/cafeteria benefits
Supported by a narrow positivist base	Supported by a wider pluralistic knowledge base

Source: Wilson and Iles, 1999 [1996], p. 31, reproduced with permission

Other commentators try to link or synthesise the two approaches. The Institute for Personnel Development (IPD, 1996) saw diversity as a vision for achieving equal opportunities (Maxwell et al., 2001). Thomas and Ely (1996) suggest that EO compliance is a part of diversity. For these commentators, equal opportunities is a subset of diversity or vice versa. However, such a position can only be maintained if, as suggested, there is no conviction that the underlying paradigm in relation to 'difference' is fundamentally dissimilar. What may be complicating distinguishing between the two approaches is the fact that the actions that result from both approaches are similar. For example, awareness training, collecting and monitoring figures on representation, support for people with particular needs such as providing a room in which to practise their religion, are likely to appear in organisations espousing either approach.

To summarise, a number of positions in relation to the two approaches appear in the discourse:

- EO and diversity are different in paradigm and in the action that follows.
- EO and diversity are different in paradigm but the actions that follow are similar.
- EO is a subset of diversity.
- Diversity is a subset of EO.

Whatever one's position on the nature of each approach and their relation, if any, to each other, there is considerable criticism of both as failing to adequately address issues of inequity.

Critiques of equal opportunities and diversity

Dissatisfaction with equal opportunities policies and action is longstanding. It is not so much the narrower focus on three groups in society which has elicited concern. One of the groups, women, after all, is half the population. Rather, equal opportunities has been derided as 'entryism' (Davies, 1998, p. 16), that is, merely injecting more of any underrepresented group into the relevant area/level of employment without attention to an inclusive culture (Grogan, 1999). Something of a paradox lies at the heart. Having more women, BME people and those with disabilities in leadership, and particularly senior leadership positions, can be interpreted as a redistribution of power. They are no longer lesser than others. However, if this is achieved by those groups being treated the same as the dominant group and adopting their lifestyle/culture/ways of working, their own personae, choices, style have been obliterated. What they are, or were, is still lesser. The assessment of equal opportunities approaches hinges on how far those previously excluded from leadership can be seen to retain the possibility of acting as they wish, first to achieve and then to enact a leadership post. A study of BME managers in English schools found those who had achieved leadership had experienced racism on their route. They continued to experience discrimination while in post. Their position therefore remained perceived as 'lesser' by some (Bush et al., 2005). Coleman's study of women secondary school teachers in England found that some felt they had to lead in a stereotypically male way (Coleman, 2002). Women college principals in England also record experiencing sexism and the strain of adopting male work styles, particularly in terms of workload (Stott and Lawson, 1997). The insistence of equal opportunities that there must be equal representation of previously underrepresented groups is a powerful pressure towards redistribution of power, at least potentially, but it appears to come at the cost of assimilation and the homogenisation of leadership.

Diversity approaches have also been criticised. While the approach appears to be much more inclusive of people who may be treated inequitably for a much wider range of reasons, it is depicted as a far more comfortable, cosier approach which allows leaders to evade their responsibility to confront inequities in power, particularly as they relate to the groups most likely to experience discrimination:

> Adopting an MD focus may mean that the focus on power, oppression and inequality inherent in many 'radical' conceptions of EO is lost ... Many groups in the UK have indicated that they still need the concentrated focus which EO/affirmative action offers to maintain the momentum of advance. (Wilson and Iles, 1999, p. 38)

Everyone is equally valued, but this does not imply a determination to achieve equal representation, that is, a redistribution of leadership and power. Lorbiecki and Jack (2000) suggest a sequential process whereby diversity arose because it provided a more palatable means of appearing to address equality issues than prior equal opportunities approaches. If politics is essentially about the control and distribution of power, then diversity is political. It avoided previous actions designed to actually redistribute power, such as affirmative action (that is preference given to the appointment/training/promotion of people from underrepresented groups), and instead substituted much softer initiatives such as cultural awareness training. A strategy that allows leaders to appear to be redistributing power while actually doing no such thing is highly political.

Springing from the myriad analyses of the nature, relationship and effectiveness of the two approaches, both equal opportunities and diversity and inclusion have their champions, and apologists. Perhaps the most important conclusion is to acknowledge that neither approach is seen to have fundamentally shifted attitudes and practice. Both have failed to a degree. There is still underrepresentation and those from underrepresented groups achieving leadership positions still are perceived by some as 'lesser' in a variety of ways. Identifying the reasons for this may require a deeper analysis of how we conceive 'difference' and diversity.

Capabilities approaches

The discourse continues to develop, most recently with the advent of capabilities approaches to equality, based on the work of Sen (1984) and Nussbaum (1999b). The United Nations has adopted an index of quality of life based on the capabilities approach which has been mooted as the basis for an approach to achieving equality within organisations. 'An important starting point is human dignity, the dignity of individuals to live a life they value' (Gagnon and Cornelius, 2000, p.71). As expounded by Nussbaum (1999b), the approach is based on the development of three capabilities:

- basic capabilities – people's innate talents and attitudes;
- internal capabilities – the tools people have been equipped with through their education and training, such as numeracy;
- combined capabilities – the interaction between the first two and the environment which allows or does not allow the use and development of basic and internal capabilities.

This is a holistic view which posits that not only development of individuals is needed to allow them to achieve their potential, but that the environment in which they function must be appropriate to allow them to act as they wish. This does not suppose that all will make the same choices. Equal outcomes are therefore not the measure of success, as not all will take the same path.

The framework was developed in relation to entire societies rather than organisations. Nevertheless, there appear to be relevant implications for leaders of schools, colleges and universities. First, the emphasis is on all people, not particular groups. Secondly, the approach is holistic, emphasising the need for multiple strategies within the organisation and beyond. Finally, the outcome is seen not as representativeness, but as each individual being able to live a life which they value. Singh (2002) translates the intention into the need for a multi-stranded approach:

> For combined capability to succeed, the workplace needs the following:
>
> - Political freedoms (trade unions, 'choice and voice' mechanisms, access to decision making power, agenda shaping power, formal collective action).
> - Economic facilities (fair wages, equal pay and fair reward).
> - Social opportunities (access to training, to promotion, to similar treatment rather than discriminative treatment in these areas).
> - Transparency guarantees (how to get to the top in a chosen career, well designed genderfair, culturally-fair assessment centre methodology for transitions into management and senior levels, clear open scrutiny of the rules of the game and how inappropriate networks are avoided).
> - Protective security (largely legal but could include a demonstration of an employer's social responsibility actions).
>
> The aim is to deliver rights enshrined in law and policy as *entitlements* leading to equality of outcome and choice. Such an approach would therefore be multi-method, multi-domain, multistakeholder focusing on an *enabling environment*. (2002, p. 30; emphasis in original)

In this approach the synergy of multiple strands relating to the whole person's experience is vital to achieve change.

The approach can be critiqued in the same way as diversity as not focusing closely enough on those groups most likely to experience disadvantage. Nevertheless, its insistence that partial measures will not do, that human beings may experience unequal outcomes, not because of barriers, but because they so chose, is a step forward in conceptualising the goals and strategies needed.

Radical approaches

More radical approaches have emerged from feminism and anti-racism. While a full analysis of both is beyond the scope of this chapter, it is possible to briefly judge their relevance as tools for educators to bring about change. Radical feminism and critical race theory share an insistence that the nature of the response to women or to black and minority ethnic people is a permanent state that cannot be changed without considerable struggle, and certainly not by incremental steps. The meta-narrative of patriarchy is the depiction of oppression of all women because they are women, invested in the fundamental structures of society, family, sexuality, work. For change to be effected, there must be deep-seated adjustment in the relations between men and women which would be the result of elemental shifts in society. For example, women's recent increasing control of the reproductive function would be seen as having the potential to achieve escape from oppression in a way that decades of equality legislation could not begin to match. Similarly, critical race theory (CRT) critiques liberal approaches to change and depicts racism as a permanent feature of society (Decuir and Dixson, 2004). CRT castigates liberal initiatives to lessen racism as only surfacing at times when the interests of the white and minority ethnic groups coalesce. Change will be the result of black solidarity unmasking the continuing stories of racism in education (Delgado and Stefancic, 2001).

Both forms of radicalism have been criticised for their essentialism (Mandell, 1995). Writing of Canadian radicalism, Bokina (1996) suggests that the apparent postmodernist engagement with race, class and gender in fact largely ignores class and focuses on race and gender:

> In practical terms, the postmodernist trinity is a duality, race and gender: two concepts that create a divisive identity politics; two concepts with important social and political implications, but whose roots ultimately lie in aspects of human biology. Within race and gender identity politics, biology is once again destiny. (Bokina, 1996, p. 182)

Bokina's criticism is that analysis based on the biological factors of gender or ethnicity underplay the considerable other influences due to societal structure. Also, the tendency to privilege oppression related to gender or to race is seen as a weakness in both gender and race analyses, as it excludes or downgrades the experience of those who are oppressed because of other reasons – their sexuality, religion, culture:

> If, as the post-structuralists argue, experience is multiple, fractured and diverse, whose experience counts as 'real'? ... Generalizing from one point of view erases, ignores or invalidates the experiences of others. (Mandell, 1995, p. 34)

Radical approaches are therefore limited as an analytical tool to respond to diversity in educational leadership, for two reasons. First, their essentialist foundations cannot encompass the multiple characteristics which meet a response that disadvantages. Secondly, their insistence on fundamental change in society is generally outside the agency of education leaders. The latter can of course model relations between people which may influence the community, but profound adjustments in society would move beyond their realistic arena of action.

In summary – the score card to date

All the approaches discussed offer something of value and also fail to fundamentally address the complex interplay of power and position. The approaches of equal opportunities, diversity and inclusion and capabilities conceptualise difference as relatively unproblematic, to be obliterated by treating all the same or as irrelevant to accruing power as all are to be valued equally. The latter stance is accepted rhetorically in normative policies, but not the lived experience of many individuals. Despite the apparent difference in goals, all three approaches translate to similar actions in organisations. Whatever the conceptualisation, the tranche of actions in 'committed' schools, college and universities is hardly differentiated and the results depressingly similar. Underrepresentation, unequal pay, the experience of discrimination and exclusion remain. Radical approaches offer more trenchant analyses, but little in the way of an agenda for action. Chapters 8 and 9 consider in more detail the strengths and limitations of initiatives which have been taken by organisations and could be further developed. Prasad and Mills (1997, p. 12) depict the approaches to achieving greater equality as a 'showcase' but suggest '[a] host of gender conflicts, race tensions and cultural frictions lie hidden in the shadows of the showcase'. The powerhouse of continuing inequity is the deeply embedded psychological processes of human relations and communication. It is to the shadows, our response to 'difference', that the next chapter turns.

3

In-groups and out-groups: The 'outsider' experience

Delving deeper

Chapter 2 considered the pressures to respond to diversity, the way the issues have been conceptualised and policies evolved in response. It suggested that despite decades of action by committed organisations, discrimination and exclusion remain a common experience. It dealt with diversity broadly defined. However, particular characteristics tend to take centre stage in policy discourse and in practice related to the degree of anxiety they provoke in individuals and organisations. There appears to be a hierarchy of characteristics of disadvantage in terms of the attention they receive, which changes over time. At the period of writing, 'diversity' is often used synonymously with black or minority ethnic people perhaps because this aspect of diversity currently creates great anxiety. Previously, gender was the characteristic more to the fore. It may be that religion is the next to top the hierarchy. If the attention paid relates to the degree of anxiety provoked by one or more characteristics, the emotional processes involved in responding to diversity are indicated to be of importance. This chapter delves further into the emotional and cognitive processes that shape relations between individuals and thereby establish inclusion and exclusion.

The psychology of communication in the differing cultures of the world could not be fully covered in one chapter. The complexities of understanding particular cultures and the competences required to communicate effectively interculturally are manifold (Stier, 2006). For example, the degree of affectivity, how far emotion is expressed in communication, varies considerably (Trompenaars and Hampden-Turner, 1997). The chapter draws on research undertaken in Western contexts and the limitations that result in application to the very wide variety of contexts globally is acknowledged.

Emotion work

Much of the emphasis in addressing diversity has been on changing the structures and processes which create and perpetuate inequity. However, both structure and process are created by and reflect underlying, often intense emotion. Rage, confusion, anxiety are the common currency in our dealings with diverse humanity (DiTomaso and Hooijberg, 1996; Osler, 1997; Prasad and Mills, 1997; Rusch, 2004). This chapter explores something of the emotion evoked from encounters with others perceived as 'different', 'the shadows of the showcase' (Prasad and Mills, 1997, p. 12). It examines the emotional underpinning of how we create perceptions of people as 'other'. It observes the result of our dealings with 'strangers', and the impetus within human behaviour to manipulate information about them in ways that reduce anxiety and maintain a feeling of security. It analyses the mechanisms by which such security is achieved and the implications for leaders and followers. It assumes that emotions are the building blocks of attitudes to individuals and groups and therefore, in working within a diverse society, education leaders must grapple with emotion.

Loss, gain and control

Much normative leadership and management literature assumes a rational approach to assessing situations and in response taking logical actions for the benefit of the organisation and/or its clients. However, numerous writers have stressed that the platform of apparent conscious rationality floats on a sea of often unconscious irrationality. For example, Korac-Kakabadse and Korac-Kakabadse (1997) suggest that the modern obsession with target setting and performance management is an attempt to wrestle with and control the deep uncertainties and therefore anxieties of modern life. Blackmore (2004) argues similarly that the rational processes imposed on schools submerge the messy emotional engagement of teaching.

Whatever the rhetoric of rationality, action is influenced by far more than logic. Underneath lie powerful personal drivers. The impetus of each individual to maintain or better their psychological and physical state is profound. Maintaining or increasing not only physical resource but also psychological security and status are the aims (Lumby and Morrison, 2006). Relations between leaders, and between leaders and followers, in diverse contexts are therefore an intensely personal and emotional experience at an individual level. To understand how people, and specifically leaders, respond to diversity we therefore need to explore reaction at an individual level. Gudykunst (1995, p. 10) theorises that our relations with others are shaped by the fact that they are 'strangers':

> Strangers represent both the idea of nearness in that they are physically close and the idea of remoteness in that they have different values and ways of doing things. Strangers are physically present and participate in a situation and, at the same time, are outside the situation because they are members of different groups … everyone we meet is a potential stranger.

Gudykunst also points out that while everyone is potentially a stranger, strangeness is relative. Most educators habitually deal with people who are relatively similar to themselves. Those who are perceived as very different are relatively rare.

However, each encounter between individuals is also an encounter between groups. Each person will be a member of a number of groups and may wear the mantle of one or more in the perception of others. Litvin (1997) argues that diversity management categorises people, who are then perceived not as individuals but as part of a group, as 'women' or 'gays' or one of numerous black and minority ethnic groups. If diversity issues arise because people see us not as an individual but as a member of a group, then we also need to understand how groups behave and the relevance of group theory to diversity and inclusion. The interaction between people is multifaceted. At both levels, individual and group, responding to 'strangers' will involve both cognitive and affective, conscious and unconscious strategies. The mechanisms are explored further in this chapter.

So far, the discussion of the emotion connected with diversity has to some degree been simplified, suggesting only that the relative degree of strangeness may increase anxiety within relationships, but the degree of strangeness is a complex matter. There is first the relative rarity of the characteristic(s) of the 'other', the degree of 'minoritiness'. Milliken and Martins (1996, p. 5), suggest that 'the proportion of representation is likely to be an important variable in predicting the outcomes of diversity'. The degree of minoritiness matters. The more a person appears a stranger the stronger the anxiety in response. Iles and Kaur Hayers (1997) suggest that there is a curvilinear effect, that some heterogeneity has a positive effect on groups, but beyond that point, the effect is negative. If a minority appears to be growing to the point of matching or exceeding the majority group, anxiety increases. The nature of the observable characteristic(s) also matters. Milliken and Martins (1996) suggest that there is much evidence of a negative emotional reaction in response to diversity in observable attributes, but that this is stronger in relation to ethnicity or gender than to age. Stone and Colella (1996, p. 362) analyse the difference in reaction to people with disabilities, depending on the nature of the disability. They suggest that the reaction will vary along a number of dimensions: '(a) aesthetic qualities, (b) origin, (c) course, (d) concealability, (e) disruptiveness, and (f) danger'. As an example, with (a) aesthetic qualities, the degree to which the disability is seen as ugly or unattractive will influence the reaction. In the case of (f) danger, the degree to which the disability is seen to pose a threat will make a difference. HIV/AIDS, widely and erroneously feared as communicable in work settings and potentially fatal, is likely to provoke a stronger negative reaction than, say, having an artificial limb. Untangling the interrelationship of multiple variables in widely varying contexts is very challenging. Research has hardly begun to unravel the complexities in educational settings. What the discussion in this chapter so far has established is that diversity provokes both cognitive and affective responses at individual and group level. Understanding the course of these reactions is key to progressing the ability of leaders to shape their own response and to influence that of followers.

Communicating with strangers

Underlying drivers

Communication begins with unspoken questions:

> What are the implications of the event for my well being? And, how can I cope with or overcome this situation? (Stone and Colella, 1996, p. 384)

To comprehend the process of communication we therefore need to understand the underlying compulsions which are indicated by these questions. Gudykunst (1995, p. 22) draws on Turner (1988) to suggest four critical human needs:

(a) our need for a sense of predictability (or trust);
(b) our need for a sense of group inclusion;
(c) our need to avoid or defuse anxiety; and
(d) our need to sustain our self-conception.

The possible implications of communication, the potential risks and rewards, are evident. Encounters with others are satisfactory when we are not anxious because we believe we can predict how they will feel, think and act, and that their emotions, thoughts and actions will confirm us in our idea of our self and as part of the group(s) with which we identify.

Similarity or perceived similarity is likely to encourage a sense of safety. There is much evidence that perceived similarity or difference to another human influences our emotional reaction, our willingness to cooperate and our capacity to work together productively. In their review of relevant literature, Milliken and Martins (1996), while acknowledging some variation related to context, suggest that not only observable characteristics such as ethnicity, gender and age, but even non-observable differences such as time of joining the organisation, educational or functional background, can have negative effects on the job satisfaction of those perceived as different to the majority and effect the performance of groups in a number of ways. They conclude:

> The consistency of these findings suggests the presence of a systemic problem, namely, that groups and organisations will act systematically to drive out individuals who are different from the majority. (Milliken and Martins, 1996, p. 14)

Sociobiologists offer one perspective on why this is so. At a biological level, 'One well studied factor that biases toward cooperation is genetic relatedness' (Sapolsky, 2002, p. 2). Those who are related genetically or who *feel* related are more likely to cooperate with each other. The roots of the similarity attraction mechanism may be genetically wired (Simons and Pelled, 1999). We may have evolved patterns of survival which favourably predispose us towards similarity. If we feel similar to another, we may be more positively disposed towards him or her. At a more conscious level, we may find it easier to trust if perceived similarity leads us to believe the behaviour of another is predictable. It is a reasonable hypothesis, though the biological drivers of our behaviour are, of course, arguably unknowable, in that they cannot be unravelled from the socialisation processes which are overlaid by upbringing.

In contrast to the implied biological determinism suggested above, social constructionists offer an alternative perspective. Human behaviour is conceived as a result of complex interactions with history, culture, language, social networks and power relations. As a result:

> Because these relationships are assumed to be open ended and malleable, rather than rigidly defined by the causal forces of biogenetic necessity, social constructionism maintains that acts of genuine altruism are indeed both conceptually possible and inherently meaningful. (Gantt and Reber, 1999, p. 5)

The implication is a belief that we can act towards others not to bolster our own status or interests, or of those perceived as similar to us, but genuinely to support any other human being. Our attitude to others perceived as different is therefore an act of will and not biologically determined. Humans can critically analyse the influences that shape them, and act as agents to bring about change if they so wish. However, there is no suggestion that humans habitually act in the interests of others to the detriment of their own. Rather, interaction is to seek approval:

> In any given social situation, in order to secure our identity, we are unable to do otherwise than seek out the acknowledgement and approbation of the others in that social situation ... we perceive the choices set before us primarily in terms of how best to situate ourselves for social advantage by pragmatically gauging whether or not various social strategies are too risky or too costly for our purposes. (Gantt and Reber, 1999, p. 8)

Gantt and Reber therefore suggest limits on altruism. People will act to support others if by so doing they gain rewards such as approval from others and/or situate themselves to gain other advantage, for example promotion. Altruism, defined as acting purely in the interests of another, appears unlikely. Currently power is with a dominant group, largely white males. To achieve equal opportunities or diversity and inclusion, it is in effect suggested that they relinquish their dominance to achieve a more equal power distribution, for example in positions of leadership. Such action appears to require a degree of altruism. There is a longstanding debate about the nature of altruism. When those who act apparently altruistically are genetically or feel genetically related, such acts are in fact in the best interests of gene survival and therefore arguably not altruistic at all (Nicholas, 1997). For those individuals who are not closely related, i.e. those perceived as 'other', altruism is suggested to be on the basis of trust that the recipient will pay back. Applying critical race theory to education, DeCuir and Dixson (2004) argue that white educators support black and minority ethnic colleagues only when their interests coincide. Certainly much of the normative literature about diversity offers incentives based on payback of various kinds. The social endorsement of others is implied or overtly suggested. To act in certain ways is to be 'politically correct', and therefore to be approved widely within society, or more specifically to be favoured by funders and those awarding quality marks. As discussed in chapter two, measurable business gains are suggested to result, such as a wider pool for recruitment, better links to the market, ultimately, greater profit. The kinds of reward mooted seem to cover all bases. One's identity is to be confirmed as laudable in meeting social justice demands. Equally, hardnosed financial or commercial gain is to result. Such altruism is therefore metamorphosed into an alterative form of egoism and brings us back to a need to understand the process by which humans try to protect themselves and better their position.

The process of communication

Individuals enter communication with two types of uncertainty, predictive and explanatory. We cannot know how another will feel, think or behave and we cannot explain why they do. The cognitive position of uncertainty evokes the affective response of anxiety. The reaction is heightened when the interaction is with, using Gudykunst's definition, a 'stranger':

> We avoid strangers because it allows us to manage our anxiety. When we are experiencing anxiety and cannot avoid strangers, we often terminate the interaction as soon as we can. Cognitively anxiety leads to biases in how we process information. The more anxious we are, the more likely we will focus on the behaviours we expect to see, such as those based on our stereotypes, and the more likely we are to confirm these expectations and not recognize behaviour which is inconsistent with our expectations. (Gudykunst, 1995, p. 14)

Stone and Colella (1996, p. 358) define stereotypes as 'largely false "overgeneralized" beliefs about members of a category that are typically negative'. The process suggested is clear. When we can, we avoid strangers or close our interaction as soon as is feasible. When communicating we firstly categorise the individual into a particular group, and then apply generalised beliefs about the group to the particular individual. The negative implications are apparent. First, the classification itself is problematic. Individuals cannot always be easily assigned a group, even assuming stable categories of groups are feasible. The physical appearance and the social cues given by a stranger may be considerably misinterpreted when the categorisation is the work of seconds. Secondly, if beliefs relevant to the group are applied to the person, they in some sense cease to be themselves, a unique individual, and are a stereotype, a representative of the group. One might imagine that further interaction would undermine simplistic assessments about individuals, but there is a problem. Once a stereotype is assigned, then information is processed in such a way as to support the stereotype and filter out any evidence to the contrary. Speaking of reactions to people with disabilities, Stone and Colella (1996, p. 360) believe:

Once a disabled person has been categorized, the category assignments take on a master status, and subsequent information about the person is dominated by the nature of this category.

Once labelled, our thinking processes work to keep the person within the category to which they have been assigned. To do other would be to risk exposure to the dangers of uncertainty and unpredictability. Stone and Colella (1996, p. 383) suggest that emotional reactions 'are largely automatic, innate, and usually irrevocable'. An example might be fear when meeting someone with a severe physical disfigurement. They further argue that this is followed by guilt and an amplified response, more positive or more negative than is warranted. Whichever direction the amplification, communication is skewed in a way it would not be were the person perceived as more similar.

In contradiction to Stone and Colella's belief in an innate automatic reaction, Gudykunst (1995) believes that if our expectations are violated, if the perceived stereotype acts differently to what is expected, we can stop the automatic emotional and cognitive process and become mindful, that is start to consciously construct a more accurate picture of the individual, rather than simply assigning stereotypical characteristics. In summary, drawing on Gudykunst, we can posit a number of theoretical assumptions about how we communicate with others and particularly how this affects the interaction with those perceived as 'different'. Gudykunst makes seven such assumptions about the process of communication:

- Both interpersonal and intergroup factors influence all of our communication.
- The identities we use in different situations influence the nature of the encounters we have with strangers.
- At least one person in any encounter is a stranger in some way.
- Most of the time that we communicate, we are not highly aware of communication behaviour.
- We do not have sufficient intersubjective understanding to avoid misunderstandings.
- Cognitive uncertainty and affective anxiety directly influence our ability to communicate effectively.
- Uncertainty involves a dialectic between novelty and predictability and anxiety involves a dialectic between trust and fear.

(Adapted from Gudykunst, 1995, pp. 18–19)

The emotionally driven nature of communication, the psychological fragility of humans and the negative impact on those perceived as different from the majority is clear. We oscillate between fear and trust as automatic defence mechanisms which lead us to swiftly assign others, 'strangers', to a group. The characteristics of the group are assumed to be those of the individual. Our anxiety in the face of perceived unpredictability is assuaged. In short, our capacity to understand and to communicate with the infinitely complex individual human being is severely constrained.

Group interaction

If the interaction between individuals draws on categorisations of groups, then group interaction is at play, and theory related to groups, such as intergroup conflict (IGC) theory, may offer useful frameworks for understanding the experience of being perceived as 'other'. A group is defined as 'a delineated social unit with properties which can be measured and with consequences for the behaviour of its members' (Sherif and Sherif, 1953, p. 9). Group norms shape and impel the beliefs and actions of individuals into one discernible direction, that of the group. The frameworks offered by IGC theory see human behaviour as fundamentally rational; that is, players make choices by a logical calculation of their best tactic to maximise benefit within ubiquitous conflict, defined as:

> a situation in which interdependent people express (manifest or latent)   differences in satisfying their individual needs and interests, and they experience interference from each other in accomplishing these goals. (Donohue and Kolt, 1992, p. 4)

Conflict between groups can arise from 'real' needs such as competition for scarce resources, but ethnographic studies have indicated that the interests of groups often exceed achieving merely sufficient material resource. As an example of the ubiquitousness of such wider aims, one might consider those of groups which apparently have little in common with educational organisations. For example, the goals of a Tlingit clan, a group of Alaskan Native Americans, were:

(1) to secure basic resources for survival;
(2) to accumulate material wealth for security;
(3) to increase social standing *vis-à-vis* other clans;
(4) to promote privilege and prestige;
(5) to establish alliances with other autonomous clans; and
(6) to expand their resource base, wealth, and prestige sphere.
(Tollefson, 1995, p. 3)

Research amongst other groups has discovered the same imperatives for securing not only physical resources but also social status (Jackson, 1993) and social domination (Alexander and Levin, 1998). Groups may not wish just for enough, but to have more than others and to accrue status. Such aims resonate with micropolitical analyses of schools and colleges (Ball, 1987; Bowe et al., 1994; Lumby and Wilson, 2003). Demands for the inclusion of groups previously excluded from leadership roles is therefore a conflictual situation where the dominance, status and rewards of one group are being challenged by other groups.

One effect of intergroup conflict is a favourable bias towards the in-group and a negative bias towards out-groups. Rather than logical and objective assessment of the validity of others' opinion, one will tend to approve of those of one's own group and view negatively those of another. Perceptions of issues are coloured by loyalty to one's own group and hostility to other groups. Out-group hostility may be reduced if superordinate goals are mutually desired and can only be achieved by collaboration (Jackson, 1993). However, IGC theory suggests that such goals must be sustained for a considerable period, or they will have no effect. A short-term alliance to achieve common aims is unlikely to impact on long-term conflict (Jackson, 1993). This suggests that where survival is dependent on cooperation with previously excluded groups, for example where recruitment of leaders is problematic, if sustained for sufficient time, the superordinate goal, to have sufficient staff, may be powerful enough to minimise the drive for status in the current dominant group. This implies that the context matters considerably. The presence or absence of superordinate goals, for example, to recruit from previously underrepresented groups, or to connect with new markets, may considerably influence the degree to which groups increase or lessen their determination to maintain dominance over other groups (Lumby and Morrison, 2006).

The powerhouse of discrimination is therefore not the choices of individual people who are, for example, consciously racist or sexist, but rather emotional, cognitive and group processes which secure advantage for the individual or group by eliminating or devaluing 'difference'. 'People assert their group's norms of exclusion with great, even intolerably great, force' (Hardin, 1995, p. 7). This is not to deny the effect of agency or of social structures, but rather to highlight that addressing such structures will not achieve fundamental change unless the underlying affective and cognitive processes are also adjusted. Indeed, the approaches outlined in Chapter 2, designed to address agency and structure rather than underlying psychology, demonstrate the weakness of such incomplete strategies.

Looking inside education

There is far too little research on the relationship between communication, group processes and diversity in educational organisations to be able to conclude how far the theory examined in the chapter so far applies to schools, colleges, universities and other centres supporting learning. There are, however, glimpses which suggest that the theory may be helpful in understanding why underrepresentation and feelings of exclusion persist (Bush et al., 2005; Coleman, 2005a; Lumby et al., 2004). We can take as an example the *Leading Learning* project, which constructed ten case studies of different kinds of organisation in different contexts within the English Learning and Skills Sector. A number of conclusions can be drawn from this work and illustrated from comments of staff. First, in only one of the ten cases was there an embedded and consistent commitment to diversity and inclusion, reflected in the comments of staff at all levels of leadership. In this particular institution, efforts to be inclusive, not just in rhetoric but with real results, were evident at strategic and operational level, resulting in:

- an equality action plan;
- a Race Equality Action Group, which reports to the Board of Governors;
- a Diversity and Equality Co-ordinator;
- codes of practice for the behaviour of staff and students to each other;
- frequent development events in relation to specific aspects of diversity;
- universal staff entitlement to development opportunities;
- supporting networks such as the Black Managers Network.

Additionally, respondents repeatedly referred to an empowering style of leadership which encouraged people to take risks, to transfer skills learned in other contexts, to develop:

> I think the leadership that I am feeling is one that empowers you and it's a coaching type of leadership very much so and I think it is demonstrated in lots of different ways. (Middle leadership focus group)

Values were embedded not only in the strategic plans of the college but in every aspect of daily practice:

> I just think that diversity is X's [area in which institution is situated] strength anyway. I think it is so embedded in everything we do. We don't stop to think sometimes. You know it's been embedded for such a long time.

It could be coincidence that this institution was situated in one of the most diverse cities in the world, but in the judgement of the staff, it was not. The social and economic neediness, the trauma of many immigrants, above all the diversity of the community within which it was situated, enforced a focus on inclusiveness:

> I think that the diversity is huge and teaching staff respond to it really well.

> I think we have learnt that because of being in X [area in which institution is situated] you have had to learn and you grow with it, you grow with the diversity.

> (First line leaders focus group)

In this institution the extremely diverse community context is experienced as a imperative to be inclusive. By contrast, in the other cases, as Milliken and Martins (1996) suggest, it is ethnicity particularly and gender to some extent which are most strongly connected by leaders with diversity. Where the community is perceived as not diverse, or 'all white', diversity and inclusion were often seen as irrelevant. One head of department expressed it in this way:

> We have a mix of male and female in my department but I don't think leadership has been influenced by gender differences. We have no ethnic minorities and so obviously that doesn't come into it. We are all quite similar in our background and upbringing, white middle-class. (Individual interview, first line leader)

Within the ten cases, in only one instance was the diversity of the community sufficient to establish superordinate goals, the recruitment of diverse staff and students
and the creation of an inclusive culture, sufficient to displace intergroup conflict.
In this case leaders were committed to the redistribution of power. In other cases,
even in two institutions where the community was relatively ethnically diverse, the
mechanisms by which individuals and groups maintain their dominance were
clearly in place.

Mechanisms of exclusion

Most leaders believe themselves to be well intentioned in relation to equity and to be
acting appropriately. However, there is a good deal of evidence that despite such
beliefs, in both the private and public sectors, employees' perceptions of how they are
treated are quite different (Bush et al., 2005; Gagnon and Cornelius, 2000; Maxwell et
al., 2001). As argued above, it is not usually leaders' conscious choices and actions
which lead to inequity and exclusion. Rather there are a number of mechanisms
which maintain dominance and of which employees may not be aware.

One such mechanism is what Foti and Miner (2003, p. 84) refer to as leader prototypes:

> Followers appear to share a set of general beliefs about the characteristics (e.g.,
> decisive, determined, intelligent) related to leadership in diverse situations.
> Furthermore, followers use their implicit theories and leader prototypes to
> decode whether or not an individual is to be judged an emergent leader.

This phenomenon was particularly strongly evident in one of the ten cases where
leaders in the focus groups referred frequently to an 'X' type of person where X was
the name of the organisation. There was clearly a mental picture of what a leader of
the organisation was like. The impetus to appoint in one's own likeness was made
explicit in another case organisation:

> When you appoint, there is a tendency to appoint one of your own, to iden-
> tify with someone, with their background or their demeanour. You think 'I
> could get on with that person'. There is no point in appointing someone you
> can't stand, but you do tend to appoint someone who is like you. If you stood
> back and said what is it we need? – I am like me. I can do that bit. I need some-
> one who is different to me, that would bring a completely different viewpoint
> to the college, it's much more challenging. It is more challenging to the team
> and to you individually to deal with someone who doesn't see things the way
> you do. (Senior leader, individual interview)

Having become a leader in followers' eyes, those who match followers' expectations
receive 'increased social power, more credit for work outcomes and greater commitment to work goals, resulting in greater effectiveness' (Foti and Miner, 2003, p.

102). It is a positive upward spiral rewarding those who match expectations and excluding those who may wish to lead differently. Such views are not surprising given the evidence that people enjoy working with others like themselves and are often more productive in groups that share similar characteristics (Milliken and Martins, 1996). This educational organisation was highly successful in terms of student accredited outcomes. Staff were long serving and tightly focused on the goal of raising achievement. There was a strong sense of solidarity which was seen as a bedrock of success and which people did not want to jeopardise by, as some saw it, risking change. On one level this was a happy and productive community of staff, well satisfied with their leadership. Giddens (1994) dismantles this cosy picture by pointing out the negative side of community; that it is generally an oppressive structure, enforcing conformity and discouraging autonomy. Staff were approved and included as long as they adopted the values and behaviour that were the norm.

A second mechanism was the perceived incompetence of the excluded (DiTomaso and Hooijberg, 1996). In the *Leading Learning* project, a questionnaire offered to all staff in the ten case organisations resulted in 794 responses. Staff were given the opportunity to make any comment they wished; 109 did so. Of these 28 (26 per cent) made a comment which both assumed addressing diversity would involve positive discrimination and criticised or rejected such assumed action. For example, the three illustrative comments below made by staff in three different organisations all imply that diversity is about the appointment of those of less ability and/or experience:

- Diversity in leadership can only be encouraged when there are suitable applicants for leadership roles.
- Appointments must be done strictly on merit and not on ethnicity or other issues of diversity. Such appointments are counterproductive and demeaning to the groups they purport to support.
- Diversity should not be an excuse to employ a person; capability is the key, irrespective of diversity issues.

The 'perceived incompetence of excluded candidates' (DiTomaso and Hooijberg, 1996, p. 180) is clearly visible in that the comments assume that to appoint more widely would involve moving away from appointment by merit.

Where people who are different from the majority are appointed, exclusion mechanisms continue. They may cluster together at break and lunchtimes (Dreaschlin et al., 2000). Those within the group see their isolation as a result of the attitudes of others. Those outside the group may see the clustering as a cause of the isolation.

The mechanisms of leader prototypes, and perceiving incompetence in the excluded result in failure to appoint diverse leaders, and the social isolation of those who are appointed. Such a picture sits uneasily with the ubiquitous upbeat commitment to equality in the mission and vision statements of schools, colleges and universities. Good schools are 'underpinned by conceptions of order and sameness' (Walker and Walker, 1998, p. 15). Whatever the rhetoric of diversity, sameness is valued and protected. Until leaders acknowledge that a much deeper understanding is needed of their own and others' attitudes, thought processes, emotions and actions, equity and diversity are as far away in leadership as they have ever been. An individual leader's well-meaning belief that they never have and never would discriminate against another is at best naïve and at worst disingenuous. Such naivety may be yet another self-protection mechanism which shields the individual from painful truths and the necessity to actually achieve greater equity, rather than merely stating this is the firm intention. There are formidable forces at work to drive out diversity. Leaders will need to grapple with strongly felt emotions and profoundly embedded processes of communication and interactions to achieve change.

In summary – how to move on?

Having established the deeply embedded processes which offer barriers to diversity and inclusion in education, we return to the practical question of how change can be achieved. One significant question is whether we can hope to theorise issues and responses generically across all the human characteristics that might be deemed 'other', or whether a focus on each of those characteristics which are most likely to meet with discrimination is more helpful. Chapters 4 and 5 turn to this issue and review the research on gender and ethnicity in education. They also consider what might be gained or lost by focusing on gender and on ethnicity as sole characteristics, rather than responding to diversity broadly.

4

Focusing on gender

Diversity is both a broad and a contested concept, but this chapter focuses on one important strand of diversity, that of gender, to consider how this aspect of diversity relates to the acquisition and practice of leadership. Chapter 5 similarly takes a specific focus, but on ethnicity and leadership. These two aspects of diversity were the initial foci of equal opportunities legislation in the UK (see Chapter 2) and it could be argued that historically the discourses of equal opportunities and social justice have developed particularly through these areas.

In Chapter 2 we argued that the discourse of diversity has roots in a business imperative and in ethical considerations. The diversity perspective is seen as qualitatively different from (although perhaps parallel to) the equal opportunities perspective, but as stressing the celebration of difference and focusing on the individual. The body of conceptual and empirical literature relating to gender can be used to illustrate generic issues of discrimination and otherness and the challenges posed to leadership by diversity. Feminist theory in particular has provided a different lens through which to observe social relations, and therefore added to our ability to conceptualise in relation to diversity and leadership. The concept and understanding of diversity are enriched by consideration of the different types of feminist thought encompassing liberal ideas of equal opportunity and more critical approaches to society and its power structures, particularly the meta-narrative of patriarchy. They have also included the somewhat essentialist valuing of 'women's ways' (Marshall, 1997, p. 12) which developed the idea of celebrating the 'difference' of women. Feminism has also incorporated the influences of postmodernism and post-structuralism, including the use of discourse analysis and concern with individual and with multifaceted identities. Nussbaum (1999b, 2002) has adopted a feminist stance in relation to the capabilities approach arguing for a new international concentration on the difficulties faced by women. Whatever the stance of the individual, feminists are united in seeing society from the point of view of 'the other' and therefore seeing the inherent injustice in social relations and the bias towards the dominant group. Feminists have therefore critically evaluated relationships and social structures that might otherwise be taken-for-granted aspects of the status quo. In doing so feminist theory has opened the way for the development of further critical and emancipatory work applicable to all dimensions of diversity.

We have singled out gender as an aspect of diversity to act as an example, to illustrate some of the wider implications of diversity and 'otherness' as it relates to leaders and leadership. However, we will also consider the specific issues related to gender and the extent to which it might be appropriate to address them separately rather than considering only a generic approach to diversity.

In this chapter we will first look at how gender impacts on the diversity of leaders, and the limited access of women to leadership, and then move on to consider how gender affects the practice of leadership. The latter part of the chapter considers how gender might inform leadership for diversity and also whether the concept of diversity can encompass gender or whether there is a case for the continuing emphasis on gender as a single example of inequity. In illustrating how gender impacts on the diversity of leaders and leadership, particular use is made of research data focusing on the impact of gender on female and male head teachers (principals) in schools in England over a period of years from 1997 to 2004 (Coleman, 2002, 2005a), allowing some comparisons to be drawn over time. The leaders who are the subject of this research are a subset of educational leaders, but the issues that are illustrated have resonance with findings on gender and leadership in other geographical areas, in other phases of education and in organisations other than education.

The 'maleness' of leadership

Although gender is just one of the ways in which individuals can be marginalised when it comes to accessing leadership, it is arguably the most pervasive, both through time and across national borders. The issue of access to leadership positions may be looked at from a simple equal opportunities point of view, taking the attitude that if the barriers to accessing leadership can be overcome through legislation and 'good practice' gender equity problems will be solved. However, whilst legislation is necessary, it is not sufficient to overcome cultural influences, including that of patriarchy, to ensure equity for women (or any other marginalised group). Feminist theorists take a critical approach to society where success is based on being a (white, middle class) male. Where a job carries prestige, social and cultural pressures ensure that it is more likely to be held by a man than a woman. In a study of male primary school teachers in New Zealand, Cushman (2005, p. 14) states that the low status of teaching 'is inextricably related to society's traditional perception of work involving children as being the role of women, and the work of women being historically undervalued and underpaid'. In most countries, the majority of teachers are women, and the more prestigious job of principal tends to be held by men (Coleman, 2002, 2005a). There are exceptions to this, but where women are in the majority as principals the status of the post is likely to be lower than in other countries. For example in Jewish schools in Israel the majority of principals are women, but the power is seen to have migrated from the schools to the administrative regional level, where men predominate as leaders (Goldring and Chen, 1994). In contrast, in the Arab sector of Israel, for cultural and economic reasons teaching is a relatively prestigious job and it follows that most teachers are therefore men (Addi-Raccah and Ayalon, 2002).

Internationally, the only area of education where most leaders are women is in early years provision, where gender stereotypes or sensitivities about child abuse may mean that men meet prejudice. As a result of these perceptions very few men become early years or infant teachers (Cushman, 2005). However, where men do venture into this area they are likely to be successful. Cameron (2001), in a review of literature on men working in childcare in the UK, USA, Australia and Scandinavia, was able to note: 'Men, it can be concluded, do well, both financially and in terms of work opportunities, when they do "women's work"' (p. 439). The tendency is for men to rise to the top even when they are in areas of female-dominated work. Men entering primary teaching in England, for example, are likely to reach a senior post. In the nursery and primary sector 16 per cent of teachers but 38 per cent of head teachers are men (DfES, 2004).

The stereotype of male leadership

Some at least of the continuing bias against women as leaders is likely to be linked to the persistent stereotype that leaders are male while women may be perceived primarily as carers and therefore as outsiders in the field of leadership. Ross-Smith and Kornberger (2004) have undertaken an analysis from Descartes, via Weber to the present day, of the philosophical and sociological links between rationality and masculinity, seeing this link as fundamental to management: 'it is the link ... between masculinity and rationality that ensures and sustains gender inequalities on all levels' (p. 299). Research undertaken by Schein (1994) through the 1970s to 1990s has shown that stereotypes of leadership and management continue to be equated to stereotypical masculine characteristics for subjects of both sexes, all ages and across continents. In addition there are structural and cultural barriers, sometimes linked to these stereotypes, that impede the progress of women to positions of power and influence. These include structural barriers within the work context and cultural expectations in society that women will take the majority of the responsibility for families and the domestic sphere. As a result of these factors, women are both seen as less appropriate as leaders in a work situation and also need to find ways of combining paid work with the main responsibility for home and family. Studies of leadership and gender in education in a range of countries across the continents have identified similar issues of stereotyping and structural difficulties (Acker, 1994; Adler et al., 1993; Blackmore, 1989, 1999; Coleman, 2002, 2005a; Collard and Reynolds, 2005; Davies, 1990; Evetts, 1994; Grogan, 1996; Hall, 1996, 1997a; Kruger, 1996; Ouston, 1993; Ozga, 1993; Ruijs, 1993; Schmuck,1996; Shakeshaft, 1989). A recent and vivid example from Australia is provided by Sinclair

(2004, p. 9), who, reflecting on her own teaching of leadership in Business Schools, identifies an archetype of leadership:

> In the Australian case, the archetype is of the lone frontier settler who is stoic, but resolute in the face of hardship. Such an image renders improbable a garrulous, emotionally expressive or more collectively oriented leader – women and many migrants from more group-based societies instantly struggle to earn respect in this context.

An illustration of perceptions of women as not appropriate for leadership can be found in the 2004 survey of principals, where half the women were aware of resentment and/or surprise from peers, colleagues and others in finding a woman in the position of head teacher. In particular those that come from 'outside' the school tended to be patronising. These include governors, parents and other visitors such as builders, although male teachers and male head teacher colleagues may also share an expectation that the head teacher 'should not' be female. Some of the women heads' perceptions include a stereotype of a traditional, authoritative male head against which they feel they are measured. A woman head in her forties commented:

> I was constantly challenged by male colleagues in the early years of headship and even described by a governor as 'a mere slip of a girl'. Members of the local community expressed their doubts as to whether I would succeed in the headship.

Women as 'outsider' leaders are also judged differently from men:

> Within my LEA, there are situations in which I have had to push for the needs of my school and am seen sometimes as difficult where a male head is seen as firm and assertive, but I can live with it! (Woman head, early fifties)

Apart from countering these gendered stereotypes, there is a range of difficulties that women may experience in the workplace if they wish to be promoted.

Impediments to women as leaders in the workplace

In the last decades of the twentieth century there were many studies that recognised that work and life was highly gendered and looked at reasons why women were less likely than men to become senior leaders in education. These studies, reviewed in Coleman (1994), identified organisational factors of overt and covert discrimination at the time of appointment and in relation to promotion. For example, women were being stereotyped into 'caring' pastoral roles that were then not seen as fitting them for senior leadership roles. Women were then 'blamed' for their lack of progress as they were seen to lack confidence in applying for promotion and were relatively hesitant in making career plans. The issue of their domestic responsibilities as well as providing practical obstacles to promotion added to the stereotype that they are not equipped for the tough job of being a leader. Although many of these studies were located in the UK, USA, Canada and Australia, similar experiences have been reported in a range of different cultures and countries. For example, Addi-Raccah and Ayalon (2002) in relation to Israel, Chisholm (2001) in South Africa, and Morris (1999) in Trinidad and Tobago.

Looking at these issues in light of the survey of women and men head teachers in the UK in 2004 (Coleman, 2005a) and comparing with the data from the 1990s (Coleman, 2002), it seems that the underlying issues particularly in relation to discrimination at appointment and the problems arising from a combination of work and family remain. In 2004, half of the women secondary heads said they had experienced discrimination in relation to applications and promotions. Commonly, interviewing panels were concerned that domestic responsibilities might impact on their ability to do their job. In 2004, it appears that there is still a perception of a clear preference for male leaders, echoing the research of Schein (1994):

> I overheard governors talking at an interview saying that I could not get the job as they needed a man on the staff! I didn't get the job. (Woman primary head, late thirties)

In view of these relatively common experiences, perhaps it is not surprising that women appear to be less likely to plan careers that include senior roles, and to have less confidence in applying for promotion than their male colleagues. Young women middle managers engaged in the English National College for School Leadership course *Leading from the Middle* (Coleman, 2005b, p. 5) showed both a lack of clear career planning, identifying only the smallest of promotions as their ambition, and a belief that men are preferred for senior posts:

> If you are interviewed I think (I don't know why) the bloke gets the job, it's the confidence the presence, how we perceive people to be rather than what they are. It is a perception, someone will walk in – the impression is he will be able to deal with this, manage this.

Difficulties in accessing promoted posts are still likely to be affected by a climate where potential employers, such as governors, are perceived to prefer men and this is exacerbated by the very real addition of domestic responsibilities to the role of many women.

Domestic responsibilities

The second wave of feminism of the 1970s and 1980s exposed the issue of unpaid work undertaken by women, and contributed to raising awareness of women's abilities and rights to take part in work outside the home. Based on British Social Attitudes Surveys 1989, 1994 and 2002, Crompton et al. (2003) indicate how women's labour force participation has changed over time, particularly for those with a child under 5 years old. In 2002 women's participation in the workforce in the UK was 72 per cent, a rise from 66 per cent in 1984. However, for women with a child under five the participation rate of 48 per cent in 1990 had risen to 57 per cent in 2001. Within this context of change, their research showed that there has been much less change than expected in the sharing of domestic work: 'women still carry out a disproportionate amount of domestic tasks and childcare. Men, however, tend to claim that they have assumed a greater share in domestic labour than is reported by women' (p. 182). They go on to conclude that work–life stress is particularly acute for women in professional and managerial occupations even though their working conditions are better than those in routine occupations. The main reason for the additional stress is seen to be the lack of domestic support that the equivalent professional and managerial men normally experience.

These findings are borne out in the 2004 survey of head teachers in England which showed that women heads who have children are likely to take more responsibility for childcare than either their own partners or their male colleague heads. In three-quarters of the households of the men head teachers, their wives or partners take the major responsibility for all domestic matters, whilst the partners of women heads take major responsibility in only just over 30 per cent of the homes. Women head teachers were still likely to be working a 'double shift' (Acker, 1994, p. 18), particularly when they had children.

A corollary of this is that many women do not choose to aspire to headship or to other senior posts because of the difficulties of combining such a responsible job with raising children. Those who are ambitious may defer their career. For example, an older woman candidate for *Leading from the Middle* stated that: 'in terms of promotions I stopped looking at anything else when I had kids'. But she had now returned to actively pursue her career. Others identified the difficulties that women with children can face in schools in terms of work–life balance.

As an alternative to deferring promotion some women may find that they wittingly or unwittingly prioritise their career over family. In 2004 women secondary heads were considerably less likely to have a partner and to have a child or children than their male colleagues (63 per cent women and 90 per cent of men). There was a greater incidence of divorce amongst women secondary heads (11 per cent of women and 2 percent of men), which may indicate a greater toll of work on their marriage. Interestingly, a study of female superintendents in the USA (Grogan, 2004) indicated that whilst many of them felt 'strongly supported by their partners in managing family responsibilities' a significant number of their marriages had ended in divorce. Chisholm (2001, p. 396) comments on the traditional division of responsibilities in South Africa and the culture of long working hours for the Gauteng Department of Education, which acts to the disadvantage of women:

> Although men felt the tension between work and home as did women, none of them had to carry domestic responsibility – if they did, this was something they chose. In stark contrast with the women, all of them managed to come

to some kind of individual resolution of the problem. Although they all recognised the issues and understood them, they also had all ensured stable domestic environments, which supported their work. That they understood the issues appeared to make no difference whatsoever to the organisational culture, or to the constructs of leadership which framed behaviours.

A way in which women may try to overcome being seen as outsiders to leadership is to try twice as hard to conform to the male model of career and the perceived male model of leadership. The stereotypical male model of career involves putting work first at all times, and women may strive to combine this attitude with having children. For example, Smithson and Stokoe (2005, p. 160) talk about 'doing macho maternity': in extreme cases women were taking off less than two weeks for maternity leave. The example is of women bank managers, but women head teachers in both surveys (Coleman, 2002, 2005a) made similar points, including comments on taking off the minimum time for maternity leave through timing their babies to be born in the summer holidays. A woman secondary head in her late forties commented in 2004 that she was 'personally determined that other staff would see my 110% commitment so my children probably suffered'.

This chapter reviews both the impact of gender on the diversity of leaders and also reflects on how gender may affect the practice of leadership. The next section outlines how gender may impact on leadership practice, particularly in a policy context that is increasingly focusing on targets and accountability although against a background of the normative approval of transformational styles of leadership (Leithwood et al., 1999).

Gender and the experience of leadership

Reference was made earlier to the valuing of the ways in which women work (for example Noddings, 1988). Although important in terms of the development of feminism, there is an inherent danger in stereotyping or 'essentialising' women as being caring and nurturing just as there is a danger in stereotyping men as hard and aggressive. It is clear that women do not all operate in one way and men in another (for example Blackmore, 1999; Coleman, 2002; Gold, 1993; Hall, 1996). Whilst the traditional identification of leadership with stereotypical male attributes continues and is influential in public perceptions, these stereotypes are not helpful to women, as they define women's leadership as a deficit model. There is actually a contradiction involved here, as feminine styles of leadership are more in keeping with those styles that now gain general approval, for example, the transformational leadership style (Leithwood et al., 1999) and other more collegial and collaborative approaches.

Reay and Ball (2000, p. 151) identify the complexities of women taking on a leadership role in a predominantly male world (e.g. secondary schools):

when women managers take up the tasks of the new role and bring gender identity and behaviour to bear, there is no simple, essential playing out of fixed gender behaviour and relations, but rather a process of accommodation and mutual acceptance.

They also comment on the need to explore the extent to which women leaders in schools in particular may be seen as mother figures, incorporating nurturing qualities but also being potentially powerful and disciplinary figures.

The surveys on men and women heads in England do indicate that men and women see themselves as operating in broadly similar ways. Their responses cannot be divided along essentialist lines (Coleman, 2002, 2005a). The norm identified by both sexes is presumably one to which most men and women head teachers aspire and is, in stereotypical terms, a relatively 'feminine', 'nurturing' style of management. It has been suggested that men's public avowal of the 'feminine' qualities could be a way in which men continue to maintain their advantage in leadership (Blackmore, 1999).

Gender and current policy

The current policy context may impact more on women than men. The increased accountability of leaders in education may be particularly hard on women, who are more likely to be noticed and held up to public scrutiny as a result of their outsider status as leaders. Moreau et al. (2005, p. 40) interviewed women teachers in England who 'all pointed to increased bureaucracy, demands for accountability – to pupils, parents and the state – and described the ways in which they felt their occupation had become driven by the need to demonstrate measurable outcomes'. In this climate, where their status as heads is questioned anyway, it is likely that women leaders will be seen as especially responsible for problems. In the 2004 survey of head teachers (Coleman, 2005a) over 70 per cent of women secondary heads felt that they had to prove their worth as a woman leader. This was 10 per cent more than in the 1990s. Comments from women leading schools in special measures and in other challenging circumstances indicated how exposed they felt in their leadership role as women.

Although men were less likely than women to say that they felt they had to prove their worth, the proportion who did so had also increased from the 1990s. A managerialist context that stresses accountability, rules and regulations and is driven by market demands affects all those in positions of responsibility but may be particularly inimical to women, discriminating against them through the increasing demands brought about by meeting targets and competition between schools. In an extreme example of this, Chan (2004) describes a school in Hong Kong where married women simply could not manage the long working hours the school required as well as handling the demands of motherhood. Chan (2004, p. 496) reports the principal as saying:

We are a service occupation and we have to commit to our customers. If teachers only see teaching as a job and simply come to school from Monday to Fri-
day, I don't think they should be here. Today is Saturday, but you can see
many teachers still come back to work. I have told teachers that summer holidays are only for students, teachers have no holidays. If we organise a visit or
an outing on Sunday, no teacher can object to the duty.

The adoption of such an extreme version of the market ethic led in this case to
unreasonable treatment of all staff, but particularly operated to penalise women
with families. A similar culture of long working hours and their impact on women
has already been described in the South African situation, with a single mother
employed in an Education Department reporting: 'You are either there at the meeting or you are not. If you have other responsibilities and cannot be there, that's
your problem. The result is that you are simply excluded from many things'
(Chisholm, 2001, p. 395).

How can gender inform leadership for diversity?

About half of the women in English secondary schools consider that as 'outsider'
leaders their status carries benefits (Coleman, 2005a), but these benefits are largely
within the existing power structures and therefore do little to affect the status quo.
They include: the ability of women to 'defuse' a situation where male teachers, parents or pupils were angry; having rarity value; using their sexuality (e.g. flirting) to
gain something for their school, and empathising with other women, mainly mothers of pupils. Women are still seen as novelties and there is nothing here to challenge gender stereotypes or to inform the diversity agenda. However, some of the
women expressed how they experienced their gender as giving them freedom to
operate in ways untrammelled by the sort of expectations that men heads may
experience (Coleman, 1996a, 2002). In the 1990s, a woman head, talking about the
relative freedom she experienced said:

> Sometimes you can get away with things because you are a woman, because
> you are breaking new ground. I've worried about the amount of time I spend
> talking to staff, but it is one of the best ways of moving things on and giving
> them confidence. Because there is no stereotype for women [heads] you can
> be more relaxed, it is not so stressful. (Coleman, 1996a, p. 172)

Some of the same enjoyment in women's leadership and management is evident in
what Chisholm (2001, p. 398) refers to as 'maternal feminism', with some women
asserting, a 'version of the "strong woman" whose strength lies in her leadership
qualities derived from motherhood'. Similarly, in describing female principals in

Trinidad and Tobago, Morris, (1999, p. 347) mentions that 'the values and beliefs that they brought with them to the task of managing their schools stemmed from their family influences as well as their educational and life experiences'. She interprets their attitudes through reference to the 'ethic of care' (Gilligan, 1982; Noddings, 1988).

These more positive attitudes to difference may therefore hold promise for some reconcepualistion of leadership and for the diversity of leaders. There is the refreshing possibility that women and others can 'break the mould' of leadership. An indepth study of six women principals in Canada led Fennell (2005, p. 163) to the view that:

> As the number of women leaders and executives continues to grow, we can expect to see further challenges to the traditional views and practices of leadership.

While men head teachers are more likely to be expected to conform to male stereotypes of leadership, expectations of women are different, meaning that they may experience freedom to act outside the norms and develop their own style. However, it should be possible for individuals – women and men – to lead and manage in ways that they see as morally right, despite the pressures of public policy.

Gender stereotyping can stultify the dynamism of leadership as a concept. Feminist post-structuralism leads us to consider the dominant discourses of gender identity, summed up by Brooker and Ha (2005, p. 19) as the categories we use to understand social life, social structures and power. They go on to say that the way of countering the control of these discourses 'is to disrupt gender binaries altogether, and advocate more complex, shifting and nuanced choices for individuals – not simply to reverse or overturn existing gender roles' (p. 19). This focus on the complexity of identities is helpful in countering blatant stereotypical responses to leadership, but if we shift the focus away from gender *per se* towards diversity we may lose sight of issues that are basic to the wellbeing of half the population.

Gender or 'diversity'

The changes in the status of women resulting from the waves of feminism during the twentieth century are giving way to a growing belief that gender discrimination and the problems associated with gender are now things of the past, that these battles have been won and that we are living in a post-feminist age where feminist critique is of historical interest only. Allied to this is a backlash against feminism, with the majority of women unwilling to attest to being feminist (Oakley, 2002). However, although there is a belief that gender equity is no longer an important issue, paradoxically most women do still recognise that injustices towards women may exist. In research carried out for the Equal Opportunities Commission (EOC),

Howard and Tibballs (2003, p. 7) concluded that:

> Although there was little support for the idea that women, as a group, are unequal in society today, paradoxically, most women respondents felt that they had experienced discrimination, either directly or through family and friends. This is particularly true for young women, and women with families at home. The main concerns are a lack of support to combine work and family roles, and sexism – in their working, personal and social lives. Yet most women were reluctant to talk about these experiences as inequalities. Women may have less well paid jobs, or do much more domestic work, but people see this as a result of individual choice and natural gender differences, rather than bias in society as a whole.

Some of the 2004 women respondents appeared to be capable of holding conflicting views, i.e. stating that they had not experienced discrimination whilst recalling actual examples of how they had experienced it!

The backlash against feminism has been mapped in Canada and Australia by Gaskell and Taylor (2003, p. 161), who identify that public and government attention is being focused in the early years of the twenty-first century on other aspects of inequity and diversity: 'the women's movement was losing its visibility on the public agenda, as attention turned to issues of difference – particularly relating to race and sexuality'.

As the term 'diversity' is being used to encompass gender, it is also being used to relate to the need for flexible working practices for all, rather than just for women. This use of the term diversity means that gender issues of inequality are being blurred as attention is shifted away to 'organizational and policymaking discourses that what is needed is more recognition of the diversity of flexible working styles and work–life balance needs, rather than policies which specifically enable working mothers to manage paid work and family needs' (Smithson and Stokoe, 2005, p. 149). Their research in banking and accountancy showed how gender-neutral language is actually used to cover up the underlying issues of gender inequality, focusing attention on the need for flexible working for all, whilst still holding on to very gendered views of work and equity issues. There is a superficial avowal of equality between men and women, but in practice, career breaks and the attendant career difficulties are still being identified with women. This research and the EOC findings (Howard and Tibballs, 2003) indicate that gender is still an issue in accessing promoted posts, but that there has been a rejection of gender as a problem. There is a widely held belief that society has changed sufficiently for women to be 'on a level playing field' with men, able to cope as individuals in accessing promotion working alongside men for the same goal of work–life balance. If we look more deeply below the rhetoric that claims that the problems faced by women in accessing leadership are no longer of consequence, we can still trace the beliefs about the natural place of women and men in society that continue to form barriers in work and elsewhere. Smithson and Stokoe suggest that 'the gender-neutral language of diversity and choice is not adequately addressing [continuing] highly gendered patterns of living and working' (p. 164).

The discourse of equity appears to be moving away from feminism and gender to focus on the wider concept of diversity.

In summary – gender, diversity and leadership

In this chapter we have been focusing on one particular example of diversity, that of gender. What issues has it raised for leadership and diversity generally and what is there about gender that might require separate consideration as an aspect of diversity?

In terms of paving the way for leading for diversity, feminism and to an extent research and writing about racism have shown us that there is more than one way in which to view the world, and that it is not compulsory for power to be in the hands of the white, male, middle class majority. Feminism has also indicated that there may be alternative modes of working rather than the stereotypically accepted 'male' model. Some women have exhibited leadership behaviour that breaks the mould and expressed satisfaction at the freedom that they feel as women leaders in a predominantly man's world. There are hints and possibilities of a different (diverse) type of leadership, freed from patriarchal stereotypes and focusing on people and values. However, the context of new public management and a culture of long hours of work inimical to family life make it more difficult to work towards new understandings of leadership. In particular, the climate of 'name and shame' means women and others who do not fit leadership stereotypes may feel especially vulnerable.

Feminism has also paved the way in relation to issues of social justice. Breaking down barriers for women sets precedents for other groups. However, although any 'othered' person will meet challenges related to accessing leadership roles, the career challenges associated with the home and the family do have a particular affinity to gender. Although society is slowly changing, the situation is still that women tend to take major responsibility in the home and for children. While this is the case, the world of work remains more difficult for women and even though men may aspire to equity and be positive about diversity, it is generally in their interests for the status quo to remain. In these circumstances the variable of gender may cut across other aspects of diversity and remain a separate identifiable challenge. In addition, there may be a special case to be made for women in developing countries, who are particularly vulnerable and where their individual rights might take precedence over 'the preservation of traditional cultural identities' (Benhabib, 2002, p. xii). The laudable aim of valuing minority cultural rights may then be antipathetic to the rights of women when those cultures are mostly patriarchal (Moller Okin, 1999).

The chapter has discussed and illustrated how the concept of leadership is stereotypically associated with men as the dominant sex. It is also true that leadership is linked with other attributes, for example dominant ethnic grouping and superior class. To some extent, the particular attributes will vary from one society to another, but the assumed superiority of the male will generally remain a constant.

As discussed in Chapter 1, diversity is a problematic concept. It is certainly one that is difficult to define and confine. We have seen in this chapter that it can be used in public and organisational life to mask or promote the denial of continuing gender inequalities and that there is a possibility of it being used to defend and underpin the status quo by drawing attention away from inequities that are, and continue to be endemic. However, it is also possible that gender as an issue holds centre stage, blocking progress in the wider arenas of diversity and social justice. Griffiths (2003, p. 16) exhorts us to

hold to a concern for individuals at the same time as focusing on broader issues of race, gender, sexuality, (dis)ability, religion, ethnicity, nationality, social class and any and all other differences that are systematically divisive in the society.

5

Focusing on ethnicity

This chapter focuses on ethnicity as an important aspect of diversity. Like gender, ethnicity has prominence in the discourses of equity, equal opportunities and critical theory as well as diversity. The chapter starts by consideration of the inter-relationship of the concepts of diversity and ethnicity and the ways in which educational policy has framed ethnicity, moving on to consider what we know about the experience of ethnic minority educational leaders in relation to barriers to leadership for black and minority ethnic educators, and also how ethnicity can impact on the practice of leadership. In this context the training and development of black and minority ethnic leaders is considered and the implications for understanding ethnicity as an aspect of diversity for educational leadership programmes. The chapter concludes with a brief consideration of the extent to which ethnicity can or should be considered separately from the wider concept of diversity.

Understanding of diversity and ethnicity

The current understanding of diversity owes much to the business case. The North West Change Centre of Manchester Business School (2002, p. 1) stated:

> Civil society depends on an appreciation of diversity – especially within the modern world of global communication, travel and trade. Successful societies can no longer sustain themselves if they are based on homogenous communities and are at war with those who are different from themselves.

Their case was then strengthened by concluding that: 'there is a strong correlation between a region's economic productivity and the diversity of its population'. Current concern with diversity springs not only from the business case, but also from ethical and moral grounds, as does the legislation combating racial and ethnic prejudice and discrimination.

The word 'diversity' when used in official statements is increasingly being seen as a synonym for ethnicity. For example, an English Home Office publication (Home Office Communication Directorate, 2004) entitled *Strength in Diversity* only refers to race/ethnicity and does not mention gender or class or any other aspect of diversity. Indeed it has as its sub-title 'Towards a Community Cohesion and Race Equality Strategy'. This tendency to elide the concepts of ethnicity and diversity may not be limited to England. As mentioned in Chapter 4, Gaskell and Taylor (2003) in tracking the rise and fall of feminism in Canada and Australia note that the discourse of diversity now focuses on race rather than gender.

Despite this growing use of the term diversity as a synonym for ethnicity, diversity remains a multifaceted concept and some studies have looked at the intersection of other 'strands' of diversity with ethnicity, for example gender and ethnicity (Addi-Raccah, 2005; Chisholm, 2001; Davidson, 1997). The particular difficulties faced by black women in higher education have recently been discussed (Crawley, 2006; Jones, 2006; Mirza, 2006). Although black women in the UK are accessing higher education as students, black women are rare in the ranks of academic staff and may 'fall between the cracks' (Jones, 2006, p. 145) since: 'in diversity language, race remains male and gender remains white' (Crawley, 2006, p. 181).

The intersection and impact on career development of ethnicity and gender with other variables, such as disability, age and sexual orientation, has also been considered (Powney et al., 2003). The research undertaken by Davidson (1997) took the form of interviews with 30 black and minority ethnic (BME) women leaders and concluded that they faced a 'concrete' rather than a glass ceiling. Davidson quotes Bhavnani (1994, p. 119) to illustrate the complexity of the situation that the BME women faced:

> Whilst black women's experience is specific and differentiated, it should not always be assumed to be constantly different from white women or black men. There will be similarities as well as differences depending on the contexts. Differences within the categories of black, of women and class need to be understood within the commonality. This does not mean that the effects of 'race' discrimination should be 'added' on to sex discrimination which, in turn is 'added' on to class discrimination. But as well as recognising specificity of experience, there needs to be an appreciation of the operation of the multiplicity of discrimination.

A further illustration of the complexity of diversity is given in relation to the changing political situation in South Africa. A School District Director stated:

> because the district is so diverse, depending on the context I'm in, at some point my masculinity and my race disappear because I'm a Jew. For example, in some Afrikaans schools there is a deep and profound anti-Semitism. Their experience of me was not as a white man but as a Jew. Others see me as a progressive. Another factor that has come in is age. I think the issue of identity is quite fluid depending on the context and the way people experience it. (Chisholm, 2001, p. 392)

Diversity is a complex and contested concept but so is ethnicity. In a note on terminology, McKenley and Gordon, (2002, p. 37) remind us that 'ethnicity' is now used
instead of 'race' on the understanding that there is only one race which is *Homo sapi-
ens*, but that 'political correctness' has meant that the words 'culture' and 'ethnicity'
have now replaced 'race' although the experience of perceived superiority and inferi-
ority remain the same no matter which words are used. Shah (2006a), in an examination of Muslim pupil identity in multi-ethnic schools, reminds us that: 'identity
configurations occur at individual, group, community, country or international levels, and the interplay with race, ethnicity, religion and many others is a complex phenomenon'. Gillborn (2004, p. 39) refers to 'ethnic *culture* as a genuine and vital part
of shifting and complex ethnic identities' (original emphasis).

   It appears that the concepts of diversity, ethnicity, race and culture are all 'slippery' and prone to change in usage and that this will have an impact on the way
that individuals envisage and act out their multiple identities.

Ethnicity and educational leadership and policy

It has been pointed out in Chapter 3 that discussion of ethnicity in education
largely focuses on the needs of students, with relatively little attention paid to the
ethnicity of educational staff. Discussion of the needs of the student body does
carry important implications for leadership in schools and colleges, particularly in
relation to the hidden curriculum. School and college leaders can give unwitting
messages to students and others through everyday actions which may carry messages about relative values. For example, if BME teachers are always identified with
second language issues with limited access to senior management teams important
messages are given about who is valued.

   We are living in increasingly multi-ethnic and diverse communities. In the UK,
the school census of 2004 indicates that pupils designated as coming from ethnic
minorities are just under half of primary and secondary school pupils in London,
about 20 per cent of pupils in metropolitan counties outside London and between
5 and 10 per cent of pupils in the rest of England reported in the *Guardian* in
November 2005 (Smithers, 2005). In the USA, King (2004, p. 72) refers to the changing demographics of the student population and the inevitable 'browning' of America. In Australia 25 per cent of students have a language background other than
English, but the teachers are 'over-whelmingly Anglo-Australian' (Allard and Santoro, 2006, p. 115).

   Ethnicity of pupils in the UK is now discussed within the context of diversity, but
historically was considered first in terms of assimilation and then later within the
frame of multiculturalism. Both the policies of assimilation and multi-culturalism
exist largely within an equal opportunities discourse, although multi-culturalism
does have the connotation of valuing diverse cultures whereas assimilation seeks to
weaken and reduce the impact of differing cultures. Assimilation was a denial of dif-

ference and a belief that: 'cultural differences obstructed integration' (Shukra et al., 2004, p. 189). McKenley and Gordon (2002, p. 38) point out that assimilation was based on an assumption that 'black culture is inferior and black values and beliefs [were] of secondary importance when considered against those held by dominant white groups'. This stance of assimilation and implicit condemnation was over-taken by a movement to recognise a more pluralist form of multicultural education: 'the recognition that schools were comprised of pupils from a variety of ethnic backgrounds, all of which had the right to be recognised as valid and equal' (p. 38). This latter approach probably still underpins most of the official attitude towards ethnicity and race in England at the time of writing. Although multiculturalism may be normatively preferable to the policy of assimilation, it has also been heav-ily criticised from the left, critics seeing it as 'a tokenist gesture meant to placate minority students and their communities while preserving intact the traditional curricular core of high status ('official') knowledge' (Gillborn, 2004, p. 36). Shukra et al. (2004, p. 187) have also pointed out that the current head of the Commission for Racial Equality in the UK, Trevor Phillips, has stated that multiculturalism may be problematic because it 'suggests separateness' (Shukra et al., 2004).

Most educational institutions have equal opportunities statements and many have policies relating to equity for all. However, multi-cultural approaches and equal opportunities policies can mask unwitting prejudice and may exist alongside an automatic assumption that whiteness is the norm with any deviation from that representing otherness. Gillborn (2005, p. 485) argues that the critical race scholar-ship of the USA is just as applicable to the UK and that:

> The most dangerous form of 'white supremacy' is not the obvious and extreme fascistic posturing of small neo-nazi groups, but rather the taken-for-granted routine privileging of white interests that goes unremarked in the political mainstream.

Critical race theory (CRT) therefore gives us a different stance from which to view ethnicity, racism and anti-racism. Writing about privileged students in higher edu-cation in the USA, King (2004, p. 73) identifies what she calls 'dysconscious racism' which she describes as 'a form of racism that tacitly accepts dominant white norms and privileges'. Similarly, Allard and Santoro (2006) comment on how the middle class, white student teachers they encounter in Australian higher education take their status for granted, convinced that success is down to individual effort and ignoring how 'those outside the dominant discourses may be marginalized through curricula, pedagogies and assessment practices that do not take into account differ-ent kinds of knowledge, or different approaches to learning or different values and beliefs' (p. 117). An alternative is for them to see those from different backgrounds as the 'exotic other' (p. 117), which also acts to exclude or to be seen as a deficit in an educational setting.

It is obvious from this brief overview that the conceptualisation of ethnicity and the policies and attitudes relating to it are both dynamic and contested. Also, that a discourse of equal opportunities is not sufficient to challenge unthinking and unspoken but nevertheless deeply held views about ethnicity. The fairly minimal literature on ethnicity and adults in education shows that when it comes to being a leader in education and elsewhere ethnicity both acts as a barrier to promotion and appointment and means that the BME leader will experience leadership differently to his or her white colleague.

The experience of black and minority ethnic leaders in education

The ethnicity of educational leaders is only rarely raised in academic literature, although recently in England two studies have been carried out for the National College for School Leadership (NCSL). These are Bush et al. (2005, 2006) and McKenley and Gordon (2002). Bush et al. (2005) is one of the few studies of black and minority ethnic leaders in schools based on survey material and on case studies of individual schools and leaders. The findings of these two studies and others relating to black and minority ethnic leaders will be considered further below.

Barriers to promotion and appointment

In England as elsewhere in the Western world there is clear evidence that the higher echelon and higher status jobs are held disproportionately by white males. The picture outlined in Chapter 4 indicates that women are less likely to be leaders because of deeply held, atavistic views that unconsciously equate leadership with masculinity and that these views are compounded by the additional domestic responsibilities for home and family that are still seen as naturally accruing to women. In similar ways, black and minority ethnic teachers are subject to structural discriminatory barriers in accessing leadership positions.

BME staff are poorly represented amongst educational leaders, but they are also less likely than their white peers to have entered the teaching profession. In Australia, Cruikshank (2004) found that recruits to teaching from the ranks of overseas-trained teachers (mainly Vietnamese-, Chinese- and Arabic-speakers who had been in Australia on average nine years) had met the following key problems in getting back to the teaching career that they had been obliged to abandon when they left their home countries:

> Obtaining reliable information on the recognition of qualifications;
> Obtaining advice and finding appropriate courses;
> Dealing with family, work and financial problems.
> (Cruikshank, 2004, p. 128)

However, once these problems were addressed, strategies could successfully be put in place to overcome difficulties and allow them access to the teaching profession again. The main key to success was having flexibility to respond to the range of needs rather than adopting a strictly bureaucratic approach that did not allow for people outside the mainstream.

There is a relative lack of black and minority ethnic teachers in the Western world, certainly in OECD countries such as Australia, Canada and in the UK (Cruikshank, 2004). The experience of black and minority ethnic teachers has only rarely been recorded in the UK (see Osler, 1997). Data on the ethnicity of teachers in England has only recently been published by the DfES (2004, 2005) and it shows that approximately 9 per cent of teachers were from an ethnic minority background, although in London, the overall figure was 31 per cent. However, the percentage of teachers from BME backgrounds in every area is smaller than the proportion of primary and secondary pupils that they teach. For example, in Outer London the percentage of BME teachers is 25 per cent and the percentage of BME pupils is nearly 50 per cent.

There is some evidence that BME teachers may find entry to the profession is difficult. The data collected in England by Bush et al. (2005) indicated that the BME respondents were normally in schools where there is a small proportion of teachers, but a larger proportion of pupils from BME backgrounds. This discrepancy between the proportion of BME students and BME staff who teach them is of concern for a number of reasons, for example in terms of offering role models for pupils, particularly as support staff are more likely to be of BME origin. The dominance of BME staff in subordinate roles can give strong messages and reinforce stereotypes in the educational and wider community:

> The school in which I work is very mixed ethnically, with approximately 25% African/Afro Caribbean, 50% white of many descriptions and 25% Indo Chinese, Turkish and mixed raced. In my school there are 65 members of staff. 4 teachers are from a black ethnic group, the rest are all of white backgrounds. The support staff have approximately 30% black staff and the rest are all of white backgrounds. In the past I have been asked whether I am the cleaner or a teaching assistant – people don't expect to see coloured senior staff. (Female, African, head of year) (Bush et al., 2005, p. 18)

Government statistics do not reveal the proportion of BME teachers who achieve senior status in England, but in a large scale survey relating to teachers' careers (Powney et al., 2003) ethnicity and gender were seen to have a large impact on promotion. While over a third of white males and 20 per cent of white females held a promoted post, only 9 per cent of BME males and 5 per cent of BME females held the higher status positions. The Bush et al. (2005) data arising from questions on career development for BME staff elicited the comment that: 'There is a running theme of adverse expectations that have clearly inhibited development' (p. 28). In summarising, the authors state that:

Most BME leaders also report examples of racism from senior managers, middle leaders, colleagues, LEAs parents and governors. These are sufficiently widespread to raise concerns about possible institutional racism. (Bush et al., 2005, p. 28)

Similar findings are reported in relation to the further education sector (Mackay and Etienne, 2006, p. 12), where 'black managers experience additional constraints to the progression of their careers'.

Being a black manager and leader

For those black and minority ethnic leaders who do progress, there are issues in the ways that they are perceived and treated by their role set. Although the black and minority ethnic teachers interviewed and surveyed by Bush et al. (2005) and Powney et al. (2003) were sometimes ambivalent about stating outright that they had experienced discrimination, Powney et al. (2003) found that minority ethnic teachers generally felt that they had been marginalised and 'ghettoised'; that is, placed in insecure situations often to do with special funding related to language or pastoral care, and 41 per cent of them felt that their ethnicity had been a negative factor in their career progress. In the Bush et al. (2005, pp. 58–59) study, many of the respondents gave examples of how their ethnicity had inhibited their career progress and affected their professional life:

My ethnicity hasn't enabled my career progression in any way. It's harder to network with White colleagues because as an Asian you are perceived as an outsider.

There is too much networking, nepotism, canvassing within the LEA and it is difficult for us to penetrate the networks our White colleagues have created there.

Maybe people in my school and community are subconsciously racist and would not want BME leaders for fear of what they will bring to the school.

Racism continues to be a barrier; it's an equation of power and prejudice. It is ingrained and institutionalised in our society. You are always marginalised, it is hard to progress if you do not fit into a slot.

BME head teachers are particularly exposed. Heads in the study undertaken by McKenley and Gordon (2002, p. 12) commented:

Nothing can prepare you for how you are perceived by others as a black headteacher. Your every move is scrutinised in the local media …

I came here in a position of authority and it has been difficult for some teachers to see beyond the colour of my skin.

In further education, Mackay and Etienne (2006) carried out a longitudinal study of seven black leaders over an 18-month period, revealing shared experiences of isolation and occupational marginalisation. Their study focuses on how the participants experienced their work role, feeling that they were not accepted in managerial roles by white colleagues, that their competence was questioned and that they were resented.

On a more positive note, one of the key findings emerging from the black and minority ethnic leaders studied by McKenley and Gordon (2002, p. 3) was their joy in leadership. The authors concluded that:

> School leaders from BME backgrounds had a strong desire to capture the joys of their leadership. Many of the black and ethnic minority communities represented in this study were settled relatively recently. School leaders from BME backgrounds saw that they could add their rich cultural heritage to the common wealth of all schools and in the process could play a unique role in transforming educational opportunities in this country.

Developing educational leaders

As black and minority ethnic leaders are underrepresented and face discrimination, subtle and otherwise, the issue of training and developing aspirant BME leaders is particularly important. However, the encouragement of diversity amongst leaders must mean that the training and development is not intended to re-create potential leaders from BME communities as clones of their white colleagues. Operating with the concept of diversity will involve some re-theorising of leadership so it is compatible with groups other than the white majority. In addition to the issue of ensuring that black and minority ethnic candidates are not overlooked for leadership roles, *all* leaders in education are responsible for developing the understanding and influencing the mores of young people in increasingly diverse communities. As Dimmock and Walker (2005, p. 4) put it:

> Given the multi-ethnic nature of schools around the world, leaders nowadays shoulder responsibility for shaping their organizations in ways that value and integrate heterogeneous groups into successful learning communities for all.

There are then two main issues relating to ethnicity and the development of educational leaders. One is singling out BME staff for affirmative action, or specially designed training; the other is addressing the nature of generic training for all aspirant and existing educational leaders.

Affirmative action

Affirmative action has never been a part of the legal framework in the UK, although the Race Relations (Amendment) Act 2000 does place a duty on employers to promote equality of opportunity amongst people of different racial groups. Affirmative action entails preference being given to a member of a currently underrepresented group for acceptance into education/training programmes or appointment to employment. In South Africa, affirmative action is being used to start to redress the balance for black people and, to an extent, women in employment situations. In Australia and parts of the USA affirmative action has been statutory, and has resulted in some advances for women and ethnic minorities but has also brought about quite violent antipathy and a backlash claiming that it is inequitable. Delgado (1991, p. 1224) sarcastically commented: 'Liberals and moderates lie awake at night, asking how far they can take this affirmative action thing without sacrificing innocent white males' (Delgado,1991, p. 1224), but then goes on to point out the irony of the biggest affirmative action of all which has actually been promoting the interests of those 'innocent white males':

> For more than 200 years, white males benefited from their own program of affirmative action, through unjustified preferences in jobs and education resulting from old-boy networks and official laws that lessened the competition. Today's affirmative action critics never characterize that scheme as affirmative action, which of course it was. (Delgado, 1991, p. 1225)

Affirmative action or positive discrimination seems generally to be distrusted in the UK with both women (see previous chapter) and BME staff regarding it with some abhorrence. In the Bush et al research (2005), one woman teacher of Caribbean origin stated:

> I would feel VERY AGGRIEVED if a fellow black teacher was promoted to my current level of responsibility owing to positive discrimination with a view to reflecting black role models. I have worked hard to get to where I currently am. (Bush et al., 2005 p. 32; emphasis in original)

Affirmative action is not formally sanctioned in the UK, though positive action, that is training and support to undertake preparation and application for jobs, has been embraced. In the USA where it has been somewhat institutionalised, there is a critical view that it has been operating only to ensure that small numbers of BME or women are appointed to a particular role, and that it is only tinkering with the system rather than bringing about radical change. Although affirmative action is viewed with distrust by many, its effectiveness to bring about change is inevitably limited by those who hold the power within the system where the scheme operates.

Specially designed training and development for BME leaders

The sensitive issue of affirmative action relates to the training of black and minority ethnic educational leaders who may either resist or welcome training that is specifically offered to them on the basis of their ethnicity. An evaluation of a course in London specifically for black and minority ethnic middle leaders (Coleman, 2004) included the following comments which indicate the ambivalence of BME participants to the focus on ethnicity and special training for BME leaders.

> You don't want to dwell on race, but how can you have such a course and not include it? I would like race to be explored. Issues have to be seen as multi-faceted, class issues and gender are important too. (Coleman, 2004, p. 12)

It was seen as absolutely vital that the participants be presented with successful black role models. One respondent commented:

> [This is] the sort of thing that inspired individuals – 'I've never seen six black heads [principals] in a room together before' – it gave people hope, and that made a lot of difference. That combined with professionalism. ... The strength of the programme was that it was not about race ... (Coleman, 2004, p. 12)

The Bush et al. (2005) research found two distinct categories of response to customised leadership development. Those that wanted customised support and those who opposed it as 'either patronising, inappropriate, or would be likely to cause further resentment within the profession' (p. 66). Within this range there was, however, a recognition of the relative commonality of BME leadership experience, the benefits of mentoring, and, as in the evaluation above, the importance of having black and minority ethnic role models for present staff and for the pupils they are teaching.

A respondent to the Bush et al. (2005, p. 68) research commented on the importance of the commonality of experience:

> I have met several other BME leaders having taken part in the Equal Access to Promotion course run by the National Union of Teachers and the National College for School Leadership. Until then, I was unaware that there were so many other people in a similar situation to mine. They too were not presently being encouraged, being given the correct tools to progress and not seen as part of the school's social culture.

The challenge of enlarging the numbers of black and minority ethnic leaders in higher education has been taken up in a number of cases. In the University of Bradford, (Archibong, 2005) senior (white) leaders/managers within the university are being paired with BME staff to offer personal 'mutual' learning and have been encouraged to discuss difficult and sensitive issues in pairs and in the whole group. While at the London South Bank University (McCaffery, 2005) a mentoring project aims to raise the expectations of women and black and minority ethnic leaders. In further education, Mackay and Etienne (2006, p. 26) argue for individuals having targeted programmes, with approaches that 'review the structural imbalances within organisations that handicap black leaders' experiences of work' as well as mentoring, secondment and work shadowing.

Generic leadership development relating to ethnicity and diversity

The training of black and minority ethnic leaders may help to ensure that the imbalance in the ranks of educational leaders is improved, but all leaders, particularly those from the dominant white, male middle class ranks need to be aware of and understand issues of diversity and ethnicity. In particular it is important in that there is a relevant component in higher education or national training programmes for educational leadership. In reviewing leadership programmes in the USA, Rusch (2004, p. 15) reports that:

> Although individuals enrolling in graduate leadership programs may come from diverse and dynamic communities, as students they frequently experience minimal coursework related to diversity or complex community cultures ... they may also find faculty less than interested in or committed to multiculturalism, cross-cultural leadership, or the education of minority children.

The same criticism of leadership programmes could be applied in the UK. A review of a major NCSL programme for middle leaders (Coleman, 2005b) indicated that the programme did not cover equity issues in any way and that there was an unspoken assumption that the programme was directed at the mainstream of potential leaders so that gender and ethnicity, for example, are not directly addressed or discussed in this large and influential training programme. In considering the challenges posed to educationalists operating in a multi-ethnic society, Shah (2006a) stresses that 'educational leaders need to create a culture of genuine mutual interest and respect, and a *belief* of being valued among all ethnic groups'. In a study of schools with at least 10 per cent of ethnic minority pupils who were obtaining average or above GCSE results, Blair (2002, p. 184) concluded that 'real anti-racist transformation taking place in the cultures of English schools required head teachers who were strong enough to lead change in the face of both overt as well as subtle forms of opposition'. In such circumstances the environment is one where 'minority ethnic group students feel psychologically safe' (2002, p. 190).

It would therefore seem to be vital that all potential and actual leaders in education are exposed to knowledge and the opportunities for growth in understanding of both the obvious and the more subtle impacts of ethnicity and other aspects of diversity. We will consider this further in Chapter 8, where we look at possibilities for change and moving forward.

In summary – the relationship between ethnicity and diversity

This chapter and Chapter 4 on gender have deliberately focused on a single aspect of diversity and posed a question about whether there is a case for looking at the single attribute rather than the totality of the wider concept.

In the case of gender, there is concern that if the concept of diversity subsumes and includes gender it might lead to the neglect of particular inequities that still face women, particularly at a time when feminism is unfashionable and unpopular (Howard and Tibballs, 2003). However, the concept of diversity recognises and celebrates the differences within communities in a way that the discourse of equal opportunities does not. To this extent the concept encompasses both the experience of women educational leaders with their potential to subvert and bypass the masculine stereotype of leadership, and also the joy of the BME leaders in both triumphing against the odds and adding to the cultural heritage of their schools. The experience of both women and of BME leaders opens up possibilities of new conceptualisations of leadership.

The discourse of equal opportunities encompasses the deficit model of assimilation, which positions cultures other than the predominant Western model as lacking. To this extent the concept of diversity which embraces the range and richness of difference is to be welcomed. However, the other and potentially subversive face of the concept of diversity is that it blunts and minimises the dangers/wrongs that are attached to both gender and ethnicity and to other areas of inequity. The concept of diversity does not easily encompass the type of criticality that is found in feminism or in critical race theory, which gives us a different basis on which to see and understand society. Moving from a focus on ethnicity or gender may mean losing that critical edge.

6

Leadership Theory and Diversity

Critiquing theory

Theories of leadership (and management) have been subject to critique for some time from the perspective of those who consider they do not adequately engage with social justice and address issues related to diversity. This chapter will review the ways in which the theory has been challenged and consider how it might be developed further to support an inclusive leadership.

Considering first the extent of research on which we might draw, there is a very large body of literature on educational leadership and a much smaller body relating it to diversity. The relationship between the two is tenuous. It is illustrated by DiTomaso and Hooijberg (1996) in relation to the generic literature as two adjacent triangles (Figure 6.1). The literature on aspects of diversity dribbles though a narrow entry into the margins of the body of literature on leadership.

The fragile relationship between the two kinds of literature is evident. Research and literature about diversity is indicated to affect only a fraction of that on leadership, the bulk of which is situated at a metaphorically distant point. DiTomaso and Hooijberg further point out that while directly addressing diversity is relatively infrequent in the literature on leadership, equally social science literature on equality/inequality rarely focuses on leadership as a concept of central influence in relation to equity.

Leadership, for the most part, has been unchallenged in its assumption of a homogeneous leadership. One exception is the sustained and developed critique of leadership theory constructed in relation to gender, as discussed in Chapter 4 (Blackmore, 1999, 2006; Coleman, 2002; Davies, 1998; Hall, 1996, 1997a; Ruijs, 1993; Shakeshaft, 1989; Sinclair, 2000). Irby et al. (2001), in an overview of the development of the generic literature which is the basis of much educational leadership theory, detail the ways in which the latter is inadequate from the point of view of women. They conclude that the conceptualisation of leadership is through a male perspective and that the effect of such theory is to create barriers to the entry of women into leadership roles and to undermine their practice when they arrive. Blackmore (2006) reviews the history of educational leadership theory's relation to social justice and feminism. She traces the intersection between global policy changes, their political and economic effects and the engagement of

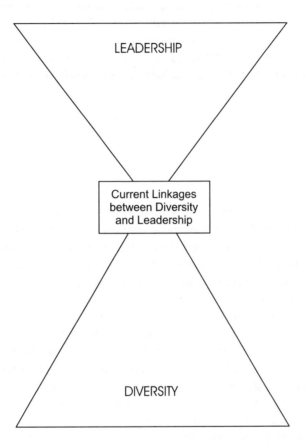

Figure 6.1 Diversity and leadership: broadening the middle (DiTomaso and Hooijberg, 1996, p. 163, reproduced with permission)

educational leadership with issues of gender and race. She concludes that 'mainstream administrative theory' lacks the conceptual frameworks and language to address the oppression of groups within education (2006, p. 191).

Critical race theory has also critiqued hegemonic notions of leadership, suggesting that the voice of minority ethnic educators is absent in its creation (Gillborn, 2004; Lopez, 2003). Osler (2006, p. 140) notes the historic 'disappearing' of minority ethnic voices and achievement and the continuing inadequacy of leadership theory and practice to move from 'colonial' models of managing otherness, which is perceived as a problem.

Others have conceived the issues differently; that it is not a question of looking at leadership theory through masculine and feminine, white or minority ethnic lenses, rather it is a question of theory and practice becoming more democratic and therefore inclusive of all (Davies, 1998; Woods, 2004). This directs us to the imperative noted by Lorbiecki and Jack (2000, p. 25) to 'theorize more than one difference at once'. Feminist critique and to a lesser extent critical race theory have offered a considerable challenge to leadership theory. Nevertheless, in their historic single essentialist focus, they are inadequate for reconstructing theory to respond to the multiple identities of individuals and to be more inclusive of all current and potential leaders, whatever their characteristics. Recognition of this weakness has been evident over time but is emerging more strongly, particularly in feminist theory (Blackmore, 2006).

Intercultural issues

Although not explicitly dealing with diversity, another relevant area of literature is concerned with intercultural issues. There is recognition that educational leadership theory embodies a set of values which reflect a largely homogeneous Western culture. This has been suggested to be inappropriate in literature that is used worldwide (Foskett and Lumby, 2003). For example, Walker (2006, p. 1) questions the adequacy of theory imported from Western contexts to those where 'leadership is mediated by important cultural norms of high power, distance, a collectivist orientation, and hierarchical compliance'. As Gronn (2001, p. 404) reminds us, 'the main concern amongst commentators has been with an alleged inappropriate translation of ideas between different contexts and the potential loss of cultural distinctiveness'. The possibility that such cultural differences may exist within the leadership of schools, colleges and universities in one nation, rather than in a crossover between different nations, has not been raised in the literature. Therefore the implications of the Western-centric nature of educational leadership theory within Western nations have not been explored in any depth. The burgeoning diversity within each nation's population would logically suggest that the culture of individuals and groups within the workforce may well be as differentiated within organisations as within a continent or across the globe. The Western values implicit in leadership theory are not seen as problematic in Western countries, even though such countries may well have multiple constituencies reflecting the culture of various minority ethnic groups, immigrants from a range of countries, men and women, different social backgrounds etc. The assumption that intercultural issues relate only or primarily to the export of theory from one part of the world to another evidences an assumption of homogeneity in the anglophone nations and in the leadership theory it produces.

This chapter suggests that despite diversity-related critiques, leadership theory contributes to maintaining homogeneity in a number of ways. The chapter considers the relationship between diversity issues and existing/emerging models of leadership and looks to what changes may be needed to achieve a genuinely inclusive theory of leadership.

Theories of leadership – the old story

There are many analyses and categorisations of leadership theory which might be described as 'the old story': that is theories which are relatively longstanding. For example, commissioned by the UK National College for School Leadership, Bush and Glover (2003), drawing on the work of Leithwood and Duke (1998) and Leithwood et al. (1999), provide an analysis of different typologies and characterisations of school leadership and identify eight models:

- Instructional
- Transformational
- Moral
- Participative
- Managerial
- Postmodern
- Interpersonal
- Contingent.

As they point out, the clarity of definition for each varies, and many are overlapping concepts. Interpersonal, participative and moral leadership could be seen as vital ingredients of transformational leadership, which is, in Kotter's (1999, p. 77) succinct definition, 'establishing direction, aligning, motivating and inspiring people'. The key word is 'aligning'. Transformational leadership theory, with its emphasis on values-based inspiration, appears to be people-centred and morality-centred. We would argue that its influence is pervasive throughout much writing on leadership, and it thereby acts as a powerhouse towards suggesting alignment of values is a critical task of leadership. Related and overlapping forms of leadership, moral, participative and interpersonal, share a similar emphasis on values and reaching an agreed position. For example, participative leadership is referred to as using democratic processes to succeed in 'bonding' staff (Bush and Glover, 2003, p. 9).

Instructional leadership has a different emphasis, on the practice of teaching and learning. It has no insistence on reaching common values, other than a focus on the job for which staff are paid, to achieve learning. However, it is not currently a widely adopted model. It is criticised for being too narrowly focused and thereby ignoring the organisational change which is central to transformational leadership (Southworth, 2002). Leithwood et al. suggested in 1999 that it had 'all the signs of a dying paradigm' (p. 502).

Managerial leadership has a technical emphasis on rationality and task organisation. As such it is explicitly suggested to be inadequate unless linked to transformational leadership (Bush and Glover, 2003). Such leadership is depicted pejoratively as 'managerialist', that is, oppressive of staff and focused on external relations and systems which have their provenance in business and which essentially focus on activities other than teaching and learning (Gleeson and Shain, 1999; Randle and Brady, 1997; Shain, 1999; Simkins, 2000). The apparent absence of an agreed values base, or rather a values base which is seen as inimical to supporting learning as the central aim, is depicted as justification for widespread negative views of this form of leadership. For example, Thrupp and Willmott (2003) suggest that many educational leadership researchers and writers 'unwittingly support damaging and inequitable policy' by their apologist texts on inappropriate business-inspired techniques.

Postmodern leadership, which Bush and Glover (2003, p. 10) define briefly as celebrating multiple subjective truths and the demise of 'absolute authority', is explored relatively infrequently in the leadership literature. In its insistence that there is no single reality but multiple truths reflecting subjective perspectives, it appears to offer a theoretical frame for accepting or celebrating different positions. However, it has not been developed to generate an agenda for action. Nor is it explicitly linked with improving performance in the way that instructional or transformational leadership are. It provides a lens through which to see the world, but it does not provide a frame for responding with action. While it insists diversity of perspective and values is a permanent state, as yet there are no theoretical clues on how in practice effectiveness can be maintained through difference. The theory acknowledges differences in power and perspective, but then leaves it there. The relationship between the concept of leadership and its practice is obscure.

Other forms of leadership are additional to the typology detailed above. For example 'distributed' leadership is widely discussed and promoted. There is, as yet, little agreement on the nature of distributed leadership or how it differs from earlier models of teamwork or delegated responsibilities (Bennett et al., 2003). Spillane et al. (2004) suggest that leadership is understood as distributed practice, stretched over the school's social context. Gronn (2000) argues that leadership is an emergent property, created by the daily activity of a group of individuals. The insistence that leadership is created by the ongoing dialectic of activity of many seems to hold out the possibility of encompassing diversity within the theory. There is the potential to recognise that the different individuals within a group may bring to the composite creation of leadership different world perspectives, values and power.

Contingent leadership is not so much a distinctive theory in its own right as a recognition of the necessity to adjust leadership in relation to context. As such, it acts as a frame for the adoption of differing approaches which are, consciously or unconsciously, underpinned by particular conceptions of leadership. However, the encouragement to take account of context offers little guidance on how one does this. How would leadership differ in a very diverse team to one that is more homogenous, if at all? How would leadership be conceived? Contingency theory assumes that by the judicious adoption of one or more approaches a leadership style appropriate to the situation can be achieved. While it offers a useful reminder of the great importance context, it is inadequate in itself to support reflection on the enactment of leadership.

Of the various theories, two are currently dominant either explicitly or by implication in much writing on educational leadership. These two, transformational and distributed, are explored further in the following section.

Sameness, sameness

There are very many articles and books which explore and to some extent endorse transformational leadership (Day et al., 2000; Lieberman and Miller, 1999; Quong et al., 1998; Sergiovanni, 1993) and distributed leadership (Gronn, 2000; Harris, 2004; Spillane et al., 2004). In order to probe more deeply the relationship of these theories to diversity, it may be helpful to examine two articles as exemplars only.

The first is Gold et al.'s 2003 article, the stance in which is similar to that in many other publications. It presents to the reader '10 "outstanding principals" engaged in the "moral art" of educational leadership' in the UK (2003, p. 127). The article endorses a values-based form of leadership, which it suggests is supported by the National College for School Leadership in England. The authors suggest that 'this model of school leadership focuses on the people involved – relationships between them in particular – and requires an approach that seeks to transform staff feelings, attitudes and beliefs' (p. 128). Practice in the schools is depicted as building consensus amongst staff and it is asserted that leadership is available to everyone. The authors conclude that the schools had 'strong value systems ... shared and articulated by all' and that teamwork was a means of ensuring 'they shared the same values and adopted the same approach' (p. 131). The article reflects the deletion of difference – 'the spirit of togetherness ... the inhibition of any feeling of "them and us" ... building consensus round the discussion ... generally building agreement' etc. (p. 133) summarised as all having the same values and pulling in the same direction. The leadership is admired for being values-centred and for adopting democratic and dispersed systems. As such, it is promoted as something rather close to an ideal. This article has been selected as an exemplar only and we are using a perspective not intended by the authors. The latter are applying a widely held theory of leadership, evident in many articles and books, suggesting that achieving common values, common aims is a primary task of the leader. The article has been used as illustrative and there are many other articles and books which might have been selected.

Reconsidering transformational leadership

The work of Gold et al. (2003) is therefore but one example of how a frame of reference, transformational leadership, can come to be unquestioned and homogeneity feted. On the face of it, there is careful attention to inclusion. Consensus is built around discussion which includes all. Leadership is open to all. And yet what is communicated powerfully by the article is not the homogenisation of the staff and leadership, but the assumption that no homogenisation is necessary. Sameness is assumed as easily achieved. Values are shared. There appears to be no disagreement. The language reflects desirable elements, optimism, egalitarianism, consensus etc. The situation in each school may of course conceivably be exactly as described, but the very degree of emphasis on the achievement of unanimity, discerned on the basis of a visit of two days, communicates a sense of polemic. If this is democracy in schools, it is easy in a way that other commentators would suggest it is not (Quantz and Rogers, 1991). The interesting question from the perspective of diversity is what has happened to those perceived as 'other', those who disagreed, those whose values differed? Were there none and if so why? Or has their otherness been obliterated, apparently quite easily? There is no sense of a challenging process in reaching the point of common values, nor any question of the cost of reaching such a point. Reynolds and Trehan (2003, p. 164) deplore 'a subtle manifestation of consensus masquerading as "common interests"'. Such a masquerade disguises the deletion of difference in that 'consensus' displaces acknowledgement of differences.

The effect is rather like an optical illusion. One glance and what appears is the commonly accepted ideal of a values- and vision-driven leadership where staff are agreed on values such as (we imagine) helping all achieve their potential. Shift the angle slightly, and the picture becomes much more disquieting; schools where deletion of 'other' is disguised as values-based inclusion and democracy (Gillborn, 2004). There is an assumption of equality as a starting point, that all can contribute equally to the ongoing achievement of consensus. As Reynolds and Trehan (2003, p. 166) argue, 'to pretend social inequalities are not present, inevitably serves the interests of the dominant group'. They draw on Fraser, who suggests 'the role of critical theory should be to *render visible* the ways in which societal inequality infects formally inclusive existing public spheres and taints discursive interaction within them' (Fraser, 1994, p. 83; emphasis in the original). It is not so much a deliberate strategy that, as Fullan (1992, p. 190) suggests, headteachers 'must manipulate the teachers and the school culture to conform' to their vision. Rather, and much more insidiously, it is a widespread assumption that a common vision and set of values can be achieved, must be achieved as a prerequisite for effectiveness. The achievement of such agreement may be suggested to be essential and benign if reached by, for example, consultative rather than manipulative processes (Begley, 1994).

The key concepts are 'consensus' and 'aligned'. There is considerable evidence that leaders consistently overestimate the degree to which colleagues believe equality to be evident (Gagnon and Cornelius, 2000) and underestimate the extent of divergence in values (Gaine, 2001). There is tension between the belief of very many leaders in education that they have given due recognition to difference and worked through to a position of agreed values, 'alignment' and agreed action 'consensus', and the research evidence that such consensus or agreement is often illusory. It is naïve or disingenuous to imagine that those with less power or status usually feel able to challenge and to express differences of opinion; rather the differences may be hidden or confined within what is perceived as acceptable boundaries. Differences are assumed to be compatible rather than the contrary. If achieving values-driven alignment is the benchmark of effective leadership, and our thesis suggests this may be so, then perceptions of effective followership and estimates of readiness for leadership roles will depend to some degree on buying into transformational concepts. This is not at the level of conscious adoption of particular leadership theory. Rather, leaders, as a matter of course, embedded in the discourse, are exhorted and encouraged to match the transformational ideal of achieving consensus and alignment and assessed on the degree to which they do so.

The mechanisms promoting sameness appear layered. The schools themselves are apparently adopting a practice which depoliticises a process of reaching what might be characterised as an illusory notion of consensus. This process is then lauded by the literature, which further embeds the approval given to forms of leadership which assume reaching agreement on practice and values is desirable and possible in a staff where 'other' appears not to exist. Researchers and leaders, even when committed to equity, do not question the validity or the implications of the agreement which is prized.

The attractiveness of such a framework both to researchers and to practitioners is easy to explain. There is much evidence, discussed in Chapter 3, that sameness pays; that, at least in the short term, people who are similar work together more easily and productively than a more diverse group. The belief that being a tight-knit group contributes to good performance is evident amongst practitioners (Lumby et al., 2004; Milliken and Martins, 1996). We are not suggesting that diverse groups *necessarily* hold diverse values or aims, nor that they would necessarily disagree on ways of working. However, a significant lever within leadership theory to maintain homogeneity and to discourage diversity is the assumption that agreement is or could be unproblematically achieved. 'Other' is deleted not by deliberate intention, but simply by not registering on researchers' and leaders' radar screen.

Reconsidering distributed leadership

A second article selected as an exemplar is by Harris (2004). Again it is used illustratively, being only one of many considering distributed leadership. The evidence for the nature and effect of this model is acknowledged to be limited, but nevertheless, the article builds a case for the potential usefulness of this theory of leadership. In suggesting that leadership is embodied in a much larger and wider range of staff, it also acknowledges that not only a redistribution of responsibilities but also of power would be necessary, and that 'it would be naïve to ignore the major structural, cultural and micropolitical barriers operating in schools that make distributed forms of leadership difficult to implement' (Harris, 2004, p. 19). There is then in this article a recognition of power differences and micropolitical barriers to extending leadership, though expressed in fairly general terms. Issues of race or gender, for example, are not explicitly raised. In trawling the growing body of literature on distributed leadership, one might hope that research would be tackling such issues as intrinsic to this form of leadership. No such focus is apparent. In fact, even within the Harris article, in contradiction to the acknowledgement of important issues of difference elsewhere the article describes distributed leadership as:

multiple sources of guidance and direction, following the contours of expertise in an organisation, made coherent through a common culture. 'It is the "glue" of a common task or goal – improvement of instruction – and a common frame of values for how to approach that task' (Elmore 2000:15). (Harris, 2004, p. 14)

Despite the acknowledgement of cultural and micropolitical differences, a 'common culture' and 'common values' are again stressed as the bedrock of effective leadership.

Racism is experienced by black and ethnic minority school leaders (Bush et al., 2005). Sexism is experienced by women leaders (Coleman, 2002) but studies of distributed leadership do not take account of this fact, nor of any of the multiple experiences of being rendered 'other'. The barriers to the distribution of leadership generally receive either a cursory acknowledgement or none at all.

Transformational and distributed leadership theories, therefore, in their promotion of a model of effective leadership which 'glues' or 'bonds' staff by common values and a common culture, do not explicitly address the necessity to confront difficult issues of values or cultures that are not commonly held. Such commonality can arguably only be achieved either by ensuring no staff with different values and perspectives are appointed, or by eradicating such difference through 'consensual' processes, which, however benignly intended, demand the homogenisation of perspectives or their suppression. Equally, many commentators assume that the issues arising from the transfer of leadership theory to alternative cultures emerge only in movement across national boundaries. Whether dominant theories of leadership may be appropriate to all those within a single country, including those of different faiths (Shah, 2006b) or different ethnicity, such as the first nations or latinos/latinas of North America (Tippeconic, 2006; Valverde, 2006), remain unconsidered. In its blindness to the social, political and cultural context within which each individual may become a leader or a follower, its easy assumption of commonality, much leadership theory implies an effort of understanding is not necessary. Thereby much leadership theory inspires practice that either deletes 'otherness' or renders it likely to be perceived as counter-productive within an organisation.

Emerging theories of leadership – the new story

The incongruity between leadership founded on common values and culture and leadership to be inclusive of diversity has been noted by others:

> The tension between sameness and difference is considerable – the political, social and cultural fabric of society between and within communities, cities, regions and countries, and so schools, is become increasingly diverse … School leaders are under constant pressure to cope with these multiple values positions. Simultaneously, however, they are pushed towards structures and practices and norms which devalue diversity and difference and continue to value

'sameness' ... These forces for sameness prevail despite widespread rhetoric to the contrary. (Walker and Walker, 1998, pp. 9–10)

In the view of Walker and Walker, sameness permeates ideas for what makes a good leader, a good team, a good school despite the recognition of increasing diversity. Numerous writers have taken a similar journey to ourselves in attempting to find alternative theories of leadership which would be more genuinely inclusive. Valverde (2006, p. 3) notes the emergence of 'enlightened, egalitarian or democratic' and 'soulful' (p. 4) leadership. Begley (2004, p. 4) writes of 'authentic leadership'. A USA network has coined the acronym New DEEL – democratic, ethical, educational leadership.

The ethics of leadership

These emerging theories of leadership place far more emphasis on ethics and inclusion, challenging what is seen as previous rhetorical morality, while leaders in fact 'acted more as managers of repressive institutions' (Valverde, 2006, p. 2). Begley (2004, p. 5), for example, is all too aware of 'the masquerading of self-interest and personal preference as ethical action'. Educational leaders would no doubt strongly refute these charges. Such results are certainly not what they consciously intend. And yet, a view of schools as benign places, focused on equity in learning, and working for the good of all, must deliberately ignore evidence on the differentiated and inequitable pathways of learners, and the continuing exclusion of those deemed 'other' from leadership roles (Blackmore, 1999; Bush et al., 2005; Coleman, 2002; Gorard et al., 2003; Lumby, 2006; Lumby and Wilson, 2003; Reay, 2001). As Quantz and Rogers (1991, pp. 3–4) point out, there is overwhelming research evidence that 'schools work for the very special interests of the status quo' and that 'active denial' is needed to remain ignorant of the exclusion of groups of learners and potential leaders indicated by research.

Theories which assume that differences either do not exist, do not matter or can be easily resolved essentially disguise existing power relations and dominance under the guise of being 'values-driven'. Begley challenges assumptions of broad support for notions of consensus and agreement such as 'democracy', depicting the use of such concepts as a means of avoiding differences in how they are understood. For him:

The new reality of school leadership is responding to value conflicts. This has become the defining characteristic of school leadership. (Begley, 2004, p. 15)

Authentic leadership

Begley's response is to develop a theory of 'authentic' leadership, which is 'a metaphor for professionally effective, ethically sound, and consciously reflective practices in educational administration' (2004, pp. 4–5). The stance assumes a personal struggle to find an ethical position in the context of value conflict and power conflict. The starting point is not to achieve 'consensus' but to improve self-knowledge and to understand the position of others so that practices will be not 'aligned' but mutually influential in moving towards goals which are not assumed to be identical. This is not alignment in its commonly used sense of all staff supporting agreed action. Rather, it assumes that some may not agree, may never agree, that goals may differ and that choices are based on acknowledgement and acceptance of such disagreements. Such leadership is an ongoing journey in which understanding and relations are constantly challenged and renewed. It is a concept of leadership which is much less certain and far tougher than the easy solidarity implied by some earlier theories.

Boscardin and Jacobson (1996, pp. 467–68) also take leadership theory to task:

> Sergiovanni (1993) contends that natural interdependence relies on a shared sense of belonging that develops from 'common goals, shared values and shared conceptions of being and doing' (pp. 10–11). Thus, in Sergiovanni's conception, similarity is a prerequisite for solidarity. But if similarity is central to social solidarity, what does that mean for diversity?

It is the same question that has been raised by ourselves and by Begley (2004). Boscardin and Jacobson's response is to conceptualise contiguity as an alternative way of perceiving an educational community. That is, community is predicated on continuing and accepted differences which cannot and should not be eradicated. Leadership must reflect this shift as 'an exclusive focus on similarity-based solidarity is not only outmoded, but potentially damaging' (p. 475). They specifically suggest the necessity to address racism and sexism and other forms of discrimination by continually engaging in 'emancipatory conversations' (p. 474). There is a similar emphasis to that of Begley's model on a moral stance that seeks consistently to understand different views. Here there is no assumption that a common set of values or aims is possible. Rather, actions that advantage one group are likely to disadvantage another. Consequently there is an ongoing dialectic of negotiating pathways which are never easy, never a 'common' good. The aim is that whatever path is chosen, it is with the understanding of its implications for others and for oneself.

Democratic leadership

Woods (2004, p. 4) explores democratic leadership and distinguishes it from distributed leadership. He critiques distributed leadership, which 'functions as a means of engendering compliance with dominant goals and values and harnessing staff commitment, ideas and expertise to realizing these. Democracy is instrumental and depoliticized.' A challenge is presented to the idea that distributed leadership empowers, in that a hierarchy remains, and internally and externally imposed limits to action remain. 'Democratic leadership entails rights to meaningful participation and respect for and expectations towards everyone as ethical beings' (2004, p. 4). In common with Begley, Woods stresses the fragility of a process that is striving towards an ethical position. However, no resolution is offered by either writer to the difficulty of reaching that position in a postmodern world where there is no meta-narrative of right and good, only a myriad different perspectives.

Leadership for diversity

It is necessary to understand the reasons for the persistence and dominance of theories which are founded on alignment and commonality. Psychological and political explanations come readily to hand. Chapter 3 argued that there is a profound impetus to favour those who are perceived as similar and that cognitive processes impel both avoidance of and negative perceptions of those deemed 'other'. Milliken and Martin's (1996, p. 10) meta-analysis of research on the effects of diversity notes that:

> Diversity in observable attributes has been consistently found to have negative effects on affective outcomes (e.g. identification with the group, satisfaction) at both the individual and group levels of analysis.

Working with those perceived as like oneself is more instantly satisfying and easier. It is therefore not surprising that theories of leadership that are founded on apparently achieving common values and aims have in practice appealed more to leaders. Psychologically, leadership founded on embracing difference is a tough call (Boscardin and Jacobson, 1996).

There is also the political issue of why the dominant group leaders would want to challenge a system that has previously delivered power to them. Henze et al. (2001) draw on earlier work of Willie (1987) and Norte (1999) to suggest five assumptions related to power relations (Table 6.1). Henze et al.'s position is similar to that of Begley, Boscardin and Jacobson, and Woods. The responsibility for the leader who truly wishes to support diversity is to step aside from habitual blindness and to communicate fully with those who not only may perceive things differently, but may also be oppressed by decisions taken, the values promoted, the aims adopted.

The question that arises is *why* leaders should do so. Much normative literature on diversity assumes a commitment on the part of educational leaders to diversity, equity, social justice. Supporting diversity is disingenuously promoted as unquestionably in the interests of all. The possibility that supporting diversity amongst leadership may result in a redistribution of power which will not be palatable to those who are dominant is not entertained. The suppression of negativity towards diversity has a parallel in the suppression of discussion amongst professionals of the wider picture of schools' contribution to maintaining the status quo. There is a sort of conspiracy of silence in the face of evidence that schools often put their own interests before those of learners (Schagen et al., 1996), and that staff may be hostile

Table 6.1   Power relations

1. Power, like energy, is neither good nor bad in and of itself, and it exists in some form in all people at all times
2. Asymmetrical power positions – that is, dominant and subordinate – always exist to greater and lesser extents in all relationships, but they are not static
3. We each occupy either dominant or subordinate positions of power relative to different individuals and relative to context
4. Inherent in being in the dominant position is that we are blind, to greater or lesser degrees, to the negative consequences of our power over others. In the subordinate position, on the other hand, we have insight into the negative consequences of the decisions and actions of those in the dominant role, because we are the ones who most feel their impact
5. There are responsibilities that correspond to each position of power. Specifically, those in the subordinate position have a responsibility to give voice to how decisions and actions affect them, and those in the dominant position have a responsibility to listen and respond to those in the subordinate role. When we recognise and effectively act upon these responsibilities, a symbiotic relationship that is mutually beneficial can result

Source: Henze et al., 2001, pp. 4–5; reproduced with permission

to those perceived as 'other' amongst the staff and learners, evidenced by even a cursory glance at the literature on racism and sexism in education. For example, the *Leading Learning* project in the Learning and Skills Sector explored staff attitudes to diversity in leadership. The findings suggest reservations and concerns amongst staff in the ten case studies, epitomised in the following quotations:

> Certainly I, as an individual, have real issues with going after particular under-represented groups. (Senior leaders focus group, Case E)

> I believe that diversity should be encouraged but not overencouraged. (Questionnaire response, Case D)

The quotations illustrate that not all education leaders are happy and willing to embrace diversity. Rather than the ubiquitous normative assumption that educational leaders are committed to equity, a political perspective would suggest that any attempts to redistribute power, to disturb current relations, will be met with resistance, hostility and retaliation. While a more diverse leadership has many advantages to offer, it would be foolish to ignore the potential negatives of a redistribution of power to those who currently hold it. This being the case, the strongest driver towards change is the moral issue of justice. However, Begley's (2004) analysis of how leaders approach moral and ethical dilemmas is not encouraging. Drawing on Roche's (1999) work, he suggests that the most common reaction is avoidance of the situation or suspending morality. Adopting a moral stance was the least frequent response to such dilemmas. It would seem that there is likely to be a relatively weak force for progress in achieving greater diversity amongst leaders, and that leadership theory plays its part in disguising and defusing inequities and in maintaining the status quo.

Theorising for the future

How then does leadership theory need to change or evolve in order to embrace diversity more fully? Our analysis so far does not give great grounds for optimism, given that existing prevalent theories have been shown to be psychologically satisfying and politically advantageous for the dominant group. The implication is that it would be extraordinarily difficult to change the current iterative and mutually supportive relationship between existing theory and practice. It would demand that leaders adopt a position which is uncomfortable and difficult, and to do so not just temporarily, but permanently. Part of the difficulty is that theory to support diversity can hold out no end point. Unlike transformational leadership which sees an end in the achievement of common values (even if illusory), a common vision, common goals, theory to support diversity can suggest only an ongoing struggle to negotiate between competing individuals and groups, in terms of power and world view. It would assume struggle and conflict without resolution. Indeed, the resolution of conflict would be no solution at all, merely preventing radical action and a shift of power to the oppressed (Nemetz and Christensen, 1996, p. 437).

Notions of justice

The difficulties confronting theorists of educational leadership are then rather similar to those confronting political theorists; how to establish a notion of justice through leadership when views of a common good will be plural and conflicting (Rawls, 1993). Young (2002) differentiates Rawls and Larmore's philosophies in that the former assumes that there will be pluralism and disagreement while Larmore (1996) assumes that there will not be disagreement, but simply equal value accorded to different choices; that is, people will not disagree on what it is best to do, but rather agree that there are alternative paths which are equally valid. This presents a great difficulty to leaders who must make choices with others in the face of reasonable and reasoned alternatives. Current theories of educational leadership offer little support on how to make such choices. Just as there is little engagement between literature about diversity and literature about educational leadership there is little engagement with axiological writing, and very little research on moral judgement in educational leadership (Langlois, 2004). While Hodgkinson's (1996) call to view educational leadership as a moral art rather than a technical process is largely currently accepted, as Richmon (2004, p. 351) points out, Hodgkinson's three-level hierarchy of values 'is not a framework for adjudicating between or resolving value conflicts'. For example, it will not help resolve differences amongst leaders who wish to prioritise the goal of either the spiritual or the learning needs of children. Models to reflect or guide a response to moral dilemmas are driven back to subjective judgements based on 'personal and professional values' (Langlois, 2004, p. 83). Engagement with axiological frameworks is not embedded in preparation and development programmes. Even focusing on diversity is not popular, let alone more abstract philosophy. Lopez (2003, p. 70) comments on the marginalisation of diversity and discrimination issues in the curriculum to prepare educational leaders in the USA, and the eagerness of some of his students to move on to 'the more important stuff'.

We find ourselves then in a situation where some current theories of leadership stress the likelihood of value conflict, different perspectives of right and good, different predilections for ways of achieving goals, and different power to press their point amongst individuals and groups. However, theory offers little guidance to leaders on how to make choices with others within this conflicted context. The frequent suggestion in the emerging theories of educational leadership is that leaders continue to communicate and consider/adjust their own values. Richmon questions the emphasis on introspection, on the internal struggle to reach a value position. Rather, he suggests:

> A more meaningful approach would be to dispossess school leaders of the notion that they have values per se, and to help them reflect *outwardly* on the sociocultural forces which impress those very values upon them. Rather than focussing reflective practices on the way we apparently *are*, we might be better off to consider *why* we are the way we are, and *how* we have come to be that way. And while this represents only a small ontological shift from our existing way of thinking, it potentially provides for a far more liberating and auspicious direction than the current concession-driven 'my values' vs. 'your values' view so often found in the literature. (Richmon, 2004, p. 353; emphasis in the original)

A great deal is demanded of the leaders of our schools, colleges and universities. They must understand *why* they hold their values and how this relates to the beliefs and values of others. They must grapple with surfacing difference and adjudicating choice, not to find a false notion of agreement but to ensure all are aware of the reasons and implications of the choices made. Leaders must make choices and in so doing they must look to be guided by the necessity to protect the disadvantaged, the minorities who will never have a powerful voice in instrumental democratic systems.

Such theory would also be less amenable to notions of leadership being about followers. Theory to embrace diversity would be not so much about what the leader does to or with others, as what the leader does within him- or herself. Business practice, particularly multinational business, driven by the necessity to achieve profitable work with a staff from many cultures, has perhaps recognised more clearly the changes in thinking required. Korac-Kakabadse and Korac-Kakabadse (1997) argue that corporations need a shift of frame, to abandon previous value hierarchisation and to adopt interpretive approaches to encountering and understanding multiple positions: 'There is a need to move beyond foundationalism, relativism and single epistemologies towards plural ontologies' (1997, p. 303). None of this provides a clear agenda for action. To date, the action agenda for diversity has generally included monitoring representation and providing training on equal opportunities. While this has contributed to progress to a degree, most fundamentally it acts as persiflage, giving a comforting appearance of determined action while distracting attention from attitudes and relations reflective of theory and practice which embed homogeneity. Chapters 8 and 9 consider this issue further and how action for change might be conceived.

Alternative theory for diversity presents challenges. It would acknowledge that leadership is created by the daily interaction of people and it is in their relationships that exclusion or inclusion resides. Leadership cannot be inclusive unless it addresses not only power distribution but also the ontological positions of all those who are current and potential leaders, essentially all staff. Negotiating the terrain of the other presents choices but no answers. Perhaps a useful metaphor is the idea of stewardship. Environmentalists stress the idea of stewardship as:

> the essential role individuals and communities play in the careful management of our common natural and cultural wealth, both now and for future generations. (Brown and Mitchell, 2000, p. 71)

While developed in relation to another field of leadership, the idea of stewardship has some merit in relation to education leaders. It would see their roles as essentially one of supporting and protecting a process designed to defend and harness productively the diversity of leaders and learners. Such leadership does not aim to inspire by providing a common direction. Rather, it promotes a process where the absence of common direction, common priorities, is surfaced in order to nurture difference. Choices of action rest on how far they will protect or harm diversity in its broad definition. The choice for right and good is measured against how far it will continue or dismantle the privilege of the dominant. Chapters 8 and 9 continue the discussion of what effective leadership for and with diversity might comprise.

In summary

Leaders are continually assessed, whether formally in preparation and development programmes or informally by learners, colleagues and the wider community. Concepts of transformational and distributed leadership are often implicit in the assessment. How would the alternative leadership we have depicted be assessed? How could the ability to continually question one's own position, to understand, even if imperfectly, the position of others, to make choices to adjust power, be assessed? And who would wish to be so assessed? The uncomfortable conclusion is that the market for educational leadership theory and for leadership preparation on the whole wants the comfortable, the advantageous, the certain. There is no demand for more nebulous and challenging theory which exacts engagement with racism, sexism and critiques the human capacity to create and disadvantage 'other'. Until such time as a demand is created, leadership theory will continue to be based on homogeneity and experienced positively by the dominant group as a warm coat. The warmth provided by the latter is quickly taken for granted. It intrudes into consciousness only when absent. Take the coat off and the discomfort of coldness becomes apparent. There is little evidence that leaders in education want to chance the coldness and discomfort of confronting diversity issues and much evidence that they, even if unconsciously, hug close the warmth of the coat.

7

What to do? Theorising aims and practice

Should we even try?

The previous chapter considered how theories of leadership relate to diversity. The absence of a clear framework for making choices and for action emerged. This chapter probes further the issues that face leaders in a context where, despite increasing diversity in our educational communities, leadership does not appear to have achieved inclusion. It considers the possible aims in the face of the dystopia of discrimination and prejudice which is described by many who experience and/or who research inequity in educational leadership, and has been outlined in part in Chapters 4 and 5 (Bush et al., 2005; Coleman, 2002; Osler, 1997). In response, decades of research and writing have not succeeded in creating a matching utopia, that is, an imagined future state where there is equity rather than inequity. The attempt to build theory and action in response to the multiple lived experiences of many who feel subject to inequity is problematic. The identity and experience of individuals who feel treated inequitably strongly influences their analysis of diversity issues and their suggested solutions (Dreaschlin et al., 2000). Depictions of the desired future are therefore often contradictory. Feminists, older workers, minority ethnic groups, those of different faiths might each see the ideal working environment in education quite differently. The path to reach the ideal is also unclear. The analyses of the causes of inequity in education leadership remain multiple, contradictory and uncertain. For some therefore, addressing diversity issues is not feasible, 'a fantasy' (Lorbiecki and Jack, 2000, p. 28); or even more troubling, initiatives to redress inequities result in exacerbating or embedding them deeper (Patrickson and Hartmann, 2001). In the light of such discouragement, and the absence of a fully formed theoretical framework, should we even try to address diversity issues?

This chapter attempts to answer that question. It considers how we might theorise the aims and what the implications might be for educational leadership practice. It reflects on some of the current tensions between those who believe that generic diversity approaches are a way forward and those who argue strongly that a focus on particular aspects of diversity, such as ethnicity or gender are a preferable stance. Finally, it concludes what foundations there might be for action, which following chapters explore more fully.

What are the aims?

Changed attitudes

There is no shortage of prescription for what educational leaders should achieve in order to make progress. The formulae vary from transforming staff attitudes to wholesale reform of society. For example, DiTomaso and Hooijberg (1996, p. 179) suggest the aim is to create cultures that 'tolerate, even embrace, the differences among groups despite their ethical presumptions'. Leaders are to engineer acceptance of difference, even when the attitudes or practice are predicated on different ethical values. Chapter 6 discussed the idea of surfacing difference and making choices in the role of steward. Is such an aim practical? Could we expect teachers and lecturers to accept whatever is someone else's belief and practice, even when they may fundamentally differ in their values? Foskett and Lumby (2003, pp. 15–16) suggest that 'the values of an individual or team are elastic. They can be stretched, but parameters will remain beyond which fundamental principles cannot move'. To exhort toleration or appreciation of difference without recognising limitations ignores the profound shaping influence of culture resulting in not just an unwillingness, but an inability to compromise beyond individually constructed parameters (Lakomski, 2001).

The evolution of 'appreciating difference' lies perhaps in a revolt from early equal opportunities initiatives which aimed at aiding those excluded from leadership to become as those in power and thereby achieve success, through the eradication of difference. For example, women were to be supported by positive action supposedly to acquire the confidence of their male colleagues. Maternity leave would deal with the difference between themselves and men which was deemed to considerably disadvantage them, namely giving birth to a child. The objections to such a strategy have been explored in Chapter 2. The current emphasis in relating to diversity, for example in multicultural approaches, has adopted a different approach, to recognise difference and to tolerate, appreciate, celebrate it (Baldwin and Hecht, 1995). This is often promoted as a strategy with no recognition or discussion of the degree to which the political and psychological sciences would suggest such behaviour is feasible. In fact, as was discussed in Chapters 3 and 6, such an endeavour faces profound barriers. Stone and Colella (1996, p. 383) argue that emotional responses are 'largely automatic, innate, and usually irrevocable' and link this to the negative response to visible or detected disability, particularly when it is perceived as unattractive. They point out that research has not found diversity training to be an effective means to alter attitudes. Lakomski (2001) argues that neurological patterns established over time are difficult to override, particularly as people avoid situations where they might encounter evidence that unsettles their current understandings, for example in contradiction to a stereotype. If understanding and attitudes are hard wired in this way, it offers one explanatory perspective on why exhortation and even training can prove so ineffective. Allix and Gronn (2005) adopt a similar perspective in relation to school leaders, suggesting that neuroepistemology is offering new insights into how school leaders learn (or don't). They describe the brain as operating two parallel systems: explicit memory, which stores conscious facts, and implicit memory, which stores the skills and behaviour acquired over a lengthy period and which is not consciously accessible. The latter of course would be responsible for processing affective responses to people. Allix and Gronn foresee similar issues to those raised by Lakomski in attempting to change attitudes and responses:

> Implicit learning is also slow, and requires practice and repetition over many trial events to accumulate and form. Once formed, however, this type of memory operates in a reflex-like manner, and is highly resistant to eradication, or forgetting ... implicit learning gives rise to a phenomenal sense of intuition in that subjects respond the way they do because it simply 'feels right', or natural, in the particular context in which they find themselves. (Allix and Gronn, 2005, p. 187)

Whether the perspective is drawn from behavioural science or cognitive science, the challenge implied by the call to 'appreciate differences' is very clear. Changing people's attitudes is a doubtful, complex and long-term endeavour.

Redistributed power

DiTomaso and Hooijberg (1996, p. 270) go further than recommending changes in attitudes:

> Leadership in the context of diversity requires more and greater challenges than offering support and commitment. Leadership in this context means to 'do' diversity in the origination, interpolation and use of structures ... it means to remake (or reengineer) the relationships of people in various categories to resources, power and opportunity.

If those currently without power or with lesser power than those in the dominant group are to have more power and opportunity, is this to be at the cost of those who currently hold power? What definition of power is implied? If power is the ability to shape the paths of others in your own interests rather than theirs, then power is a finite commodity. Its transfer to others must be at the expense of those currently holding power. As power transfers from, say, men to women, do the latter become the dominant group, the ones who now hold power and dominance? If so, the same issues of exclusion and domination apply but simply exerted by a different group. Such logic, based on an understanding of power as finite, suggests inequity can never be eradicated, merely reconfigured as power transfers from one dominant group to another. Those who gain power leave their subordinate position to become dominant and another group replaces them in their subordinate position. This accords with intergroup conflict theory which suggests that groups will find grounds for conflict even when they each have adequate resource and are not threatened in any way (Alexander and Levin, 1998; Jackson, 1993). Groups have a profound impetus towards competition with other groups, to accrue status as much as resource. 'The mere act of categorizing individuals into groups' (Alexander and Levin, 1998, p. 630) can lead to conflict.

Micropolitical analyses of schools and colleges support the analysis of intergroup theory; different levels of leaders, different subject areas, new staff and longer-serving staff, men and women, white and ethnic minorities, smokers and non-smokers are but a few of the groupings which may be in conflict with each other (Ball 1987; Bowe et al., 1994; Lumby, 2001). Litvin (1997) argues that diversity is founded on the categorisation of individuals into groups. Chapter 3 explored the psychological process of allocation of strangers to a group. The chain of reasoning which emerges is that individuals are likely both to perceive themselves and to be perceived by others as a member of one or more groups. Groups vie for dominance through acquisition of resources but also status. The path to equity is therefore barred by psychological and political processes which compel groups to compete. Such theoretical analyses suggest that conflict is inevitable. If such a perspective is adopted, then encouragement to appreciate or tolerate difference and to redistribute power appears merely fatuous.

Power, however, might be defined differently by some feminists as 'power with' (Arendt, 1972; Brunner, 2002; Hall, 1996). Women principals may repudiate notions of themselves holding power over, defined as using their position and influence to gain their own ends (Brunner, 2000; Smulyan, 2000). Rather, power is used to forward the interests of others, such as learners or other staff. As such, they may argue, it is no longer power, or is a different kind of power. Blackmore provides an example of one Australian principal who:

> did not feel comfortable with the notion of having power *over* others. Power was 'a male way of doing things', and professionally and ethically questionable. She redefined her power as power through and with others – shared leadership – ... (Blackmore, 1999, p. 161; emphasis in the original)

Power with assumes that power is not finite but can be stretched over more people than currently, through, for example, consensual processes. This conception 'defines power as a capacity to accomplish certain social goals through cooperation among people or groups with various interests and concerns' (Brunner, 2002, p. 699). The hope held out by feminists is that leaders may so engage a wider group that power is used 'synergistically or jointly' to achieve common ends (p. 699). Women educators therefore are depicted as wresting power from patriarchal systems in schools and colleges and then metamorphosing it when in a position of authority. Women principals therefore are debarred from power both by traditional views of what is 'womanly' and by progressive feminist views which deplore the exercise of power (Blackmore, 1999). However, Brunner points out that in her research with men and women educational leaders, the vast majority are exercising power over rather than power with. Some women appeared to be attempting a mixed model, with some use of power over and some power with. Nevertheless, the conclusion reached is that power conceived as dominance is at the very heart of current conceptions of leadership.

Conceptions of power with rest on the assumption that common ends can be agreed. Chapter 6 has explored the issue of false notions of consensus and how far a common end is possible. Blackmore (1999) takes us back to Foucault (1980, p. 95), 'Where there is power, there is resistance'. How feasible is it to assume that chosen actions may benefit more than one group, for example, both women and ethnic minorities, or those of deeply held religious beliefs as well as atheists or minority sexual orientations (Moller Okin, 2002)? There are many examples of situations where there are profound differences in belief, values and preferred practice. For example, research in equity in schools in Ireland raised the tensions in equity for gay people in a Catholic country (Morrison and Lumby, 2006). Perhaps it is learners who are to be the focus of common cause? And yet aims such as 'raising attainment for all', which appear to offer a common aim, may be a means of disguising choices of action and resource allocation which prioritise the needs of one learner group above another. Theories of power with rest on a belief that communities can act in a common cause, rather than be shaped by power struggles. Even more problematic is the belief that there can be a common cause beyond generally professed aims at the macro level. The moment general aims are translated into action and resource allocation, tensions in the relative benefits to various groups of individuals emerge. However passionately one may wish power with were possible, there is little research evidence to demonstrate the reality in education and much evidence in contradiction. Brunner (2002) acknowledges that the feminist assumption that power can be used benignly is aspirational rather than a widespread reality. Analyses which call for power distribution are dependent on the weak force of the preference of women and men who operate in a feminine style. Rather than merely redistributing power, feminists are attempting to recreate it in an alternative form, but with a recognition that in both theory and practice there are fragile foundations as yet.

Theory related to groups is not the only conceptual perspective that could be adopted. Individual perspectives are also possible. Perhaps the aim is not to replace one dominant group with another, as intergroup conflict theory would predict, but to have a mix of individual characteristics and backgrounds amongst those in leadership roles, each achieving their post by merit alone. A dominant group would persist within the school or college (for example senior leaders), but comprising a more diverse profile. Power would persist, but be redistributed amongst individuals more equally rather than belong to particular groups. Weber's (1947) theory of bureaucracy suggests exactly this; that roles should be allocated on the basis of expertise alone. However, this theoretical perspective ignores the issue of the construction of what is deemed merit or expertise. Is it possible to have a notion of merit that is not coloured by the preferences and beliefs of particular groups? In a review of the relevant literature, Foti and Miner (2003) conclude that there are accepted attributes of leaders, some of which reach across cultures and some of which are specific to particular locations. Leader emergence and persistence are dependent not just on technical expertise, but on conformity to the accepted characteristics of 'leaders'. The impact of entrenched conceptions of leadership has been discussed in some detail in Chapter 6. There is also considerable literature analysing the masculinity of such characteristics, as discussed in Chapter 4 (Coleman, 2002; Irby et al., 2002). There is less exploring the relationship of leadership to ethnicity (or other characteristics that may be met with discrimination), but some indication that black people feel excluded from paths to leadership by the necessity to conform to prototypes (Lumby et al., 2005). An equitable path to leadership would therefore be predicated on prototypes of leadership that are equally relevant and acceptable to all. The meta-analyses of attributes of leadership reviewed by Foti and Miner (2003) derive from hierarchic business organisations. It may be that retheorising educational leadership could offer some hope that leadership emergence and persistence could be related to a core of attributes which are not masculine or reflective of white/Western culture. Such a hope is perhaps as faint as the possibility of changing attitudes to avoid stereotyping. Nevertheless, it persists as a hope.

Changed structures

A number of writers relate the creation of equity to the demise or recreation of organisational structure. Foti and Miner (2003) argue that as organisations grow, they tend to transform into hierarchic organisations. Hierarchies offer privilege and status to those at the same level 'while literally subordinating all those who occupy lower levels' (Prasad and Mills, 1997, p. 19). Representation aims at privilege and status being distributed more equitably amongst different groups, but those who are 'lesser' will still remain. Rather than focusing on the distribution of status, an alternative strategy is to disassemble the structure which offers status differentially, the hierarchy. Davies (1998) argues that schools in all countries have features of bureaucracy, entailing both vertical and horizontal demarcations, and that hierarchy is strongly related to patriarchy in schools. In fact, as she points out, schools and colleges are not bureaucracies as depicted by Weber's ideal type (1947). The latter insists that roles are deployed strictly in relation to expertise rather than any other characteristic. Davies argues schools do not do this. They use 'trappings of rules and conformity in order to mask the play of power' (Davies, 1998, p. 19). Organisational structures have if anything been moving to strengthen hierarchy rather than the contrary. Analyses of the impact of managerialism in educational organisations suggest an intensification of the power differential between organisational levels (Gleeson and Shain, 1999; Randle and Brady, 1997; Shain, 1999; Simkins, 2000). Managerialism is defined as an increase in the coercive power of senior leaders predicated on their greater control of resources and greater surveillance of staff through audit and quality systems. It is also assumed to require a shift in values where learners' needs are of lesser importance than those of the organisation, where growth in the finance and status of the organisation is the primary aim. While this may present a pure type of a managerialist approach, the nature and degree of its presence in schools, colleges and universities has been contested (Elliott and Hall, 1994; Gleeson, 2001; Gleeson and Shain, 1999; Simkins and Lumby, 2002). However, there is a reasonable degree of agreement that some shifts have taken place and that these may have impacted on equity amongst staff in a number of ways. First, the increasing concentration of power in the principal/senior management, which is disproportionately male, white and able-bodied, has effectively strengthened the hold of the dominant group over organisations and increased their subordination of others. Secondly, the performativity and accountability culture which has swept education globally foregrounds and values certain approaches to leadership and management which are related to stereotypical masculine and Western characteristics. Thirdly, the constant state of fiscal and public relations crisis in many organisations is seen to require bureaucratic and hierarchic structures to supply the 'strong' management and direction which is viewed as the only antidote to organisational chaos and decline. Such management calls largely on masculine attributes.

In response to such inequities, Davies (1998) suggests that the focus should be not on redressing the grievance of particular groups, but rather on reconfiguring organisations as democracies which therefore offer power to all to shape choice and action. The aim is not 'having more "women at the top" but [by] having structures in place which promote equity' (Davies, 1998, p. 24). What such a structure might be is not specified. Woods (2004) points out that democratic structures cannot be taken to guarantee inclusion. As discussed in Chapter 6, as enacted in distributed leadership forms it can function 'as a means of engendering compliance with dominant goals and values and harnessing staff commitment, ideas, expertise and experience to realizing these' (Woods, 2004, p. 4). Woods suggests that democracy be conceived as offering rights to participate and influence decisions, to contribute to open discussion and to aspire to truth. Given the competing truths stressed in Chapter 6, the aspiration is likely to equate to a continuing search rather than ever reaching a single truth.

In summary therefore, the means by which greater equity is to be achieved are changes in attitudes of individuals, changes in the use of power and changes in structure. The ultimate aim of the change is not entirely clear. While there is rejection of representation as a single aim, alternatives remain shadowy. Gagnon and Cornelius (2000), drawing on the work of Nussbaum (1999a), suggest that individuals should be free to develop their potential and live lives they value. It is problematic to define how we might assess progress towards such an end other than through the subjective judgements of individuals. Nevertheless, such could be the aim in educational organisations applied equally to both learners and staff, including leaders. Even if not measurable in an easy numeric sense, it is a defined aim on which to judge the efficacy of approaches and processes to achieve it.

The process of change

The discussion in the chapter so far has suggested that the aim is that individuals should be free to develop their potential and live lives they value, and that the means to achieve the aim depend on changing the attitudes and practice of the dominant group and the structures which it has established. However, asking the dominant group to change what has served its interests so well can at best be seen as a doubtful enterprise and likely to meet with resistance. A Catch-22 situation results where things can change as long as the dominant group is persuaded that nothing will change, that their dominance or interests will not be compromised in any way 'that valuing diversity can become an organisational reality – for every-body – with no loss of power or privilege and no backlash' (Sinclair, 2000, p. 241). Nevertheless, utopian visions of toleration and appreciation of difference bubble up ubiquitously in normative documents on diversity. When Thomas More coined the term 'utopia' in the sixteenth century (More, 1994) it was intended ironically, deriving from the Greek for a 'good place' but also 'no place'. The concept of utopia has been suggested as a useful tool in that it provides visions of aspiration without which humanity would have seen less progress:

> A map of the world that does not include Utopia is not worth even glancing at, for it leaves out the one country at which Humanity is always landing. And when Humanity lands there, it looks out, and seeing a better country, sets sail. Progress is the realisation of Utopias. (Oscar Wilde, 2004, p. 15)

Are we then to understand exhortation towards tolerance, appreciation, celebration of difference and redistribution of power as utopian; recognised as not feasible but nevertheless providing a vision to which we aspire to move closer? While sociobiological and psychological theory does not provide many grounds for optimism in relation to changing attitudes or power distribution, there are perspectives that give some ground for hope. Gudykunst (1995, p. 16) suggests we accept anxiety and the defensiveness which follows as a given in human relations, but believes:

> Much of the time when we communicate using our implicit theories, we can control our automatic processing. That is, we can consciously decide to stop automatically processing information and start to consciously process information.

This state he calls 'mindfulness' (1995, p. 16). He suggests that any attempt to stop humans categorising others is futile. Rather, the aim is to categorise others more exactly:

> Being mindful involves making more, not fewer distinctions. To illustrate, when we are mindless we tend to use broad categories to predict strangers' behaviour, such as their culture, ethnicity, sex, or the role they are playing. When we are mindful, we can create new categories that are more specific. The

more subcategories we use, the more personalized the information. (Gudykunst, 1995, p. 16)

Focusing on the interaction, not its outcome, understanding that our messages and cues can be understood differently than we intend, distinguishing both commonalities and differences, are purposeful strategies to process information more accurately. Gundykunst concludes that the anxiety and uncertainty evoked by communication with strangers can be managed. The theory he offers is subtle and complex. It is but one example of theory which offers hope that we can make progress in relation to automatic negative responses to strangers, and that discrimination and stereotyping might be lessened. However, it is also strongly suggested that to achieve this will involve as much depth and subtlety in understanding and practice of technique as is required for classroom interactions with learners. While much theory is discouraging, some holds out hope for change, but on the basis of consistent, persistent efforts of committed leaders to simultaneously address attitudes, power and structure in their own and others' practice. Tambourine-waving calls to 'celebrate difference' are a long way off such a process.

Generic and specific approaches

As suggested earlier in the chapter, while there may be agreement on an aim at the meta level, once practical decisions must be made, disagreement surfaces. Chapter 2 discussed the emergence and history of various approaches to addressing inequity, particularly equal opportunities, diversity and inclusion and capabilities approaches. The discussion overlies a deeper struggle between theorists, practitioners and individuals about the merits of initiatives which focus on specific groups or generic approaches to diversity issues. Ochbuki and Suzuki (2003) draw on the work of Druckman (1994) and Harinck et al. (2000) to suggest three kinds of conflict issues:

- Gain/loss issues – the acquisition or loss of resource.
- Correct/incorrect issues – differences of opinion on how a task should be performed.
- Right/wrong issues – difference of opinion on underlying values.
  (Adapted from Ochbuki and Suzuki, 2003, p. 63)

In the public domain generally, and in the debate about diversity specifically, disagreement is often couched in discourses of right/wrong, that it is right to achieve equity by this means rather than that. Ochbuki and Suzuki point out that such discourse sometimes conceals gain/loss conflict. Professionalism generally precludes overt arguments based on self-interest. Rather, dialogue, while it may reflect genuinely held difference of opinion about the right way to go about achieving an aim, is sometimes also convenient camouflage for the influence of vested interests. Even in the arena of the fight for greater equity, a struggle for prominence can be perceived amongst different interest groups. Consequently, if feminists or ethnic minorities argue against diversity and inclusion as an approach, this may reflect genuinely held opinions. Alternatively, or as well, their position could be understood to reflect self-interest. The preferences of specific interest groups may reflect what they think may work best for them, not necessarily what will work best for all. Debates about the relative appropriateness and efficacy of approaches which focus on specific groups, such as feminism or anti-racism, are set against generic approaches such as diversity and inclusion. Opposition to such generic approaches reflects an unwillingness to have a particular cause submerged within a broader view of inequity. Gender and race have generally received more attention than other characteristics that may be met by discrimination. Generic approaches therefore may be perceived as losing ground for feminism and racism, or gaining ground for others who feel that some aspect of their identity has met with discrimination and provoked less concern than it should. An alternative perspective questions the effectiveness of diversity and inclusion approaches for any individual or group. As in any aspect of diversity, the dialogue is complex and political.

The arguments for preferring a generic approach to diversity are made on a number of grounds:

1 Diversity approaches are inclusive. They encompass all the characteristics that might result in disadvantage to an individual or group.
2 As diversity approaches are inclusive, they encompass the tensions between the interests of different groups.
3 Diversity aligns with the practice of managers who do not relate to 'women' or 'ethnic minorities' or 'the disabled' but work with people, each of whom may have multiple identities and an individual profile that is not easily categorised by group membership.
4 As diversity approaches are inclusive they are perceived as less threatening and so provoke less resistance and are more effective in achieving change.

In relation to the first point, Sinclair (2000) argues that diversity approaches encourage consideration of all those characteristics, including those that are not visible, which may be met with discrimination. The explanatory theory and practice required to address characteristics that are invisible may be different from that related to visible characteristics. Theory to relate to diversity can therefore be inclusive of all. In relation to point 2, Moller Okin (2002) writes of the tensions between feminism and the value accorded to what she sees as the patriarchal values embedded in some minority ethnic cultures. As a consequence, gender and ethnicity (and religion) must be considered in synthesis rather than separately. Similar arguments have been made of the necessity to consider socio-economic class in synthesis with gender, ethnicity and disability (Bokina, 1996). Points 3 and 4 are predicated on the greater effectiveness of an approach which is likely to engage rather than the contrary. There is considerable evidence of the degree to which what was perceived as the privileging of certain groups, for example though affirmative action, alienated leaders and lessened their willingness to consider diversity issues in the 1980s and 1990s (Lorbiecki and Jack, 2000). Sinclair (2002), while she deplores many aspects of diversity, acknowledges that it is much easier to get resources to embed diversity within leadership training than to get resources to address gender issues. In pragmatic terms, diversity is depicted as a more effective approach as it 'reduces backlash propensity' (Sinclair, 2002, p. 239).

In opposition to this argument, it is suggested that rather than focusing on all, diversity focuses on none, and consequently achieves little other than camouflaging a lack of radical change. Feminists argue that issues distinctive to single groups, such as childbirth/rearing, are lost in an approach which purports to be for all. Calls to 'appreciate differences' do not address, for example, the disproportionate burden of childrearing and housekeeping tasks. Some groups also argue that the order of inequity they experience is such as to justify a single perspective on their cause. Research justifies the notion of differential inequity. For example, Maznevski (1994) found that the negative affective response in the workplace is stronger in relation to women and minority ethnic people than to those who are a minority because of their age.

Both of the perspectives bring compelling points to the debate. While it might feel more satisfying to conclude that one or the other is correct, such a conclusion would in itself be exclusive and divisive. It is exclusive because it would alienate those who believe the contrary and divisive because it would split support for action. As argued earlier, diversity is complex and requires a sophisticated response rather than simplistic judgements. Gudykunst points out that some of the underlying mechanisms of stereotyping and discrimination are similar across groups, and as such it is reasonable to address such behaviour generically. He also recognises that there are distinctive issues in relation to particular groups, but that these are volatile and therefore not easily addressed by approaches focused on a single group as a homogeneous mass:

- There are various areas of intolerance/appreciation based on group belonging, including (but not limited to) 'race', sex, sexual preference, age, physical/mental ability, and socioeconomic status.
- Spheres of intolerance can be looked at collectively, as many of the underlying components are the same, or separate from one another as each has its distinctness.
- A sphere of intolerance (e.g. 'racism') may be manifested differently from culture to culture, from one point of history to another, or even within the same point in culture and history.
  (Adapted from Gudykunst, 1995, p. 70)

Gudykunst is arguing not for an either/or, generic or specific, but for both. Single groups perspectives will always offer a depth of understanding and ideas in response which are absent from generic approaches. Feminist writing, for example, is argued to advance the cause of women and potentially to change mind-sets so they are more open to other forms of disadvantage. However, their disadvantage is a propensity to both essentialise the group in question and to prioritise its needs. Feminism has dominated the discourse on diversity in educational leadership. The literature, while powerful and insightful, has done little to advance the cause of other groups, for example, those who have disabilities. While women may be subject to inequity in a number of ways, their majority status privileges them in a way that minority groups could never enjoy. A generic approach to diversity and inclusion is the overarching approach within which the needs of particular groups can receive attention.

In summary – aims and approaches

Those currently in power argue for addressing diversity to boost performance and to reduce inequity. Bryant (1998) has depicted the emphasis placed in the USA on goal clarity. Clear measurable aims and proven effective measures to achieve them are in demand. Representativeness remains the current dominant aim in education because it supplies a measurable end point and because equal opportunities initiatives can offer suggested routes to achieve it (Rusch, 2004). This and previous chapters have argued that such a single aim is unacceptable to many as it leaves untouched the underlying culture, power and structures which support inequity. An alternative is to accept that there is no one measurable aim which will achieve equity. Nor is there any single approach likely to promote it. Differences will persist between people, and though greater toleration or appreciation may be possible, there will always be limitations to what people's value systems and previous neurological/behavioural patterns can accept. Difference will persist and will not just be appreciated but also be the cause of conflict. If individuals are to be free to develop their potential and live lives they value, contiguity and conflict must be embraced. As argued in Chapter 6, leaders will need to call upon sophisticated analyses of their own and others' behaviour in order to continue to refine the choices they make to address inequity, holding in tension a generic diversity perspective and the issues of specific groups. Commonality cannot be assumed. Many choices will inevitably favour one individual or group. The most that can be hoped is that choices are conscious of such implications and constantly renegotiated and renewed. Addressing inequity in teaching and learning is an extremely complex process which leaders recognise as such. Addressing inequity in leadership is equally so. Ironically, the more complex and accurate analyses of inequity may be, the less they may recommend themselves to pressured leaders wanting quick-win solutions. Nevertheless, mindful and persistent renegotiation of relationships and choices of action are more likely to shift attitudes, power and structure than simpler surface initiatives. There is a place for the latter, but not as a substitute for deeper change.

8

Taking action

This chapter focuses on the ways in which leaders might take action in relation to the over-arching concept of diversity and/or its constituent parts. The difficulties of changing attitudes and the importance of redistributing power and changing structures are acknowledged but, to return to the position stated in Chapter 1, we recognise that leaders are in a position to influence and bring about change. They have a formal role which allows them to exercise power in ways that others cannot, and they are in a position to steer the organisation they lead towards an understanding and appreciation of the complexities of diversity and social justice. Throughout this book there have been references to the difficulties of bringing about cognitive and structural changes in relation to stereotyping and the valuing of in-groups over those that are seen as 'other'. Whilst recognising these difficulties, this chapter is concerned with the ways that leaders and leadership can change and bring about change in others. The discussion in this chapter focusing on 'the leader' recognises that there is not only one leader in an organisation, but that leadership can be exercised at the level of the sub-unit, or may be exercised by a team, for example a senior leadership team in a school or college.

The chapter explores change at the operational level, which is designed to complement and contribute to change at the cognitive and structural level, the focus of Chapter 9. Operational change has been the subject of criticism within this volume and more widely as unlikely to dent the deeper structures of inequity. We are arguing that change at this level, although futile as the only approach, has a part to play in diversity initiatives that can be promoted by leaders in education.

Taking action in relation to leadership and diversity includes the question of how to ensure that leaders are 'diverse', eliminating or at least reducing a situation where being a member of a socially privileged group means automatic advantage in accessing leadership positions. Taking action in relation to leadership and diversity also includes leading an organisation where respect for diversity is ingrained in the way that people communicate and operate. If knowledge and understanding of diversity is a vital part of leadership, there are implications for the ways that leadership is exercised and modelled to others and for the education and training of future leaders. Leaders in education and elsewhere may need to lead for diversity in ways that are not at present reflected in current theory and practice, but are different, more flexible and fluid than previously. In her book entitled *Action for Social Justice in Education*, Griffiths (2003, p. 10) poses two questions that are relevant to leaders in education:

1 How should we best live with the lovely diversity of human beings?
2 How can education best benefit all individuals and also the society in which they live?

Leaders have responsibility to address these questions: 'with the intention of providing action for change for the better' (p. 10). However, we recognise that leaders operate within a legal and political framework that contextualises and to some extent determines their attitudes and basic levels of action in relation to diversity, for example employment legislation in the UK and elsewhere affects human resource management.

Frameworks for action – liberal and critical approaches

Consideration of diversity takes place within a range of discourses and is also bounded by political and statutory considerations. Although demographic and economic pressures are linked with diversity and driven by practical and pragmatic concerns for market share and obtaining a competitive edge, in the world of education, diversity is more likely to be linked to issues of social justice, at least in the policy discourse. The field of social justice encompasses both equal opportunities approaches and views that are potentially more radical. Within these widely defined approaches a range of actions and changes are possible.

As discussed in Chapter 2, liberal approaches focus on equal opportunities to counter direct and indirect discrimination and, strictly defined, tend to assume that there is the proverbial 'level playing field'. Leadership for diversity goes further than issues of entry and access and is concerned with the creation and maintenance of a positive and inclusive culture. Broadly, the equal opportunities approach and diversity approaches both exist within a liberal tradition of respect for each individual, in the sense of: 'equal importance of each life, seen on its own terms rather than as part of a larger organic or corporate whole' (Nussbaum, 1999b, p. 10).

Liberal approaches can be contrasted with the critical stance adopted, for example, by radical feminism and by critical race theory. Gillborn (2005, p. 485) critiques 'education policy as an act of white supremacy', where he points out 'the taken-for-granted routine privileging of white interests that goes unremarked in the political mainstream'. Critical views give us fresh understanding and point to areas of privilege and inequity that might otherwise go unnoticed, enabling us to see society differently, providing us with a more incisive and uncluttered view, here expressed in relation to feminism:

Although we know that one pair of glasses does not fit all, as a culture, we are expected to use a common lens to view our world. This lens is a lens ground in the framework of the dominant culture. As a result we come to know our world through images that reflect the deeply embedded values and beliefs derived from a dominant culture of white, middle-class, heterosexual males. Other perspectives which do not reflect the norms and standards of this dominant culture become blurred or rendered invisible. (Gosetti and Rusch, 1995, p. 14)

Critical views of society help us see what is wrong but do not necessarily offer us any practical help in how to progress and improve societal and institutional injustice. On the other hand, liberal approaches offer ideas for action but generally do little to change the status quo. Nevertheless, the individual leader in education and elsewhere does have opportunities to bring about some levels of change.

Frameworks for action – legislation

The individual educational leader is operating within the implicit values and technical considerations of the legal framework of the state. Legislation regulates issues of equality and discrimination. Direct discrimination is when someone is treated less favourably, for example in relation to employment, simply on grounds of their sex or race; indirect discrimination occurs, for example, when a non-essential requirement for a job has the effect of exclusion on grounds of sex, race or disability or any other aspect of diversity where legislation applies. Legislation is predicated on a belief that it can impact on attitudes and institutional cultures, moving society towards a greater toleration and respect for all individuals The legislation of the 1970s in the UK, for example, underpinned changes in attitudes to the rights of women and ethnic minorities. Stone and Colella (1996, p. 371) claim that legislation in the USA, the Americans with Disabilities Act, will have positive effects for people with disabilities, and Nussbaum (2002, pp. 454–55) states that the Individuals with Disabilities Education Act (IDEA) of 1997:

begins from a simple yet profound idea: that of human individuality. Rather than regarding the various types of disabled persons as faceless classes of persons, the act assumes that they are in fact individuals, with varying needs, and that therefore all prescription for groups of them would be inappropriate.

However, legislation provides a necessary rather than a sufficient base for the development of social justice and respect for diversity and it is likely that the major concern of human resource managers in respect to diversity will be to avoid breaking the law. For example, keeping data on the recruitment of staff is a statutory requirement in the UK (HEFCE, 2004, p. 11) in relation to:

- selecting and training panel members;
- applications and appointments;
- success rates for the different selection methods;
- permanent, temporary or fixed-term appointments.

And because 'the burden of proof to show that discrimination has not taken place rests with the employer in an employment tribunal' (p. 19), it is recommended that data be kept in relation to the career progression of:

- staff, by grade and type of post;
- staff, by length of service;
- staff training and development, including applications and selection if appropriate;
- the results of training and career development programmes or strategies that target staff from particular racial groups;
- staff appraisals;
- staff promotion, including recruitment methods and criteria for choosing candidates.

Positive discrimination and affirmative action policies (as defined in Chapter 2), which can have a greater impact on opportunities for women and ethnic minorities, have been included in legislation, for example in South Africa. In Australia affirmative action was briefly adopted and paved the way for the emergence of the 'femocrats' in Australia (Yeatman, 1990). In some states of the USA it has led to the promotion of more women and members of ethnic minority groups. However, affirmative action is contentious, with proponents seeing it as ensuring equity for minorities and opponents believing it to be completely unfair to the majority (Moses and Marin, 2006).

The individual leader in education in the UK and elsewhere is therefore likely to approach diversity within a broadly liberal framework and in a context of legislation that seeks to prevent discrimination and ensure that technically there is equal access within the job market. For leaders in larger organisations, there may also be policies at the institutional level.

Frameworks for action – institutional policies

Recruitment policies in educational organisations take cognisance of equal opportunities legislation, but particularly in larger organisations, for example local education authorities, colleges and universities, there are often other policy statements about equity and equal opportunity. However, in general these policies in education tend to focus on students rather than staff (Deem and Morley, 2006; Mirza, 2006). Having undertaken case study research on staff experiences of equality policies in six UK higher education institutions, Deem and Morley concluded that there was a general lack of knowledge of social justice issues amongst staff, with gender and ethnicity referred to most frequently, disability mentioned rarely and then mainly in relation to students, and other forms of inequality like sexual orientation or religion apparent only to a very small number of staff. They found:

> The approach to staff inequality [which is] marked by management initiated, top-down policies, legislative and funding body compliance, a concern to avoid litigation, recognitional strategies and a celebration of organisational diversity per se. (Deem and Morley, 2006, p. 198)

The contrast with the 1980s and 1990s was noted, when union and pressure group action was seen to bring a 'radical edge and commitment to redistributive social justice' (p. 198). Writing from the point of view of a black woman academic, Jones (2006, p. 149) agrees that the adoption of equal opportunities policies has been: 'more in the spirit of compliance with legislation than from an ethical or moral sense'.

Some larger organisations have adopted policies of 'mainstreaming', which in ideal terms means that:

> Equality and diversity must be on the agenda at all levels, in every part of our organisation if it is to succeed. It cannot be a bolt on to other policies and initiatives. (Cabinet Office, 2005)

Mainstreaming means the integration of diversity throughout the organisation, but is suggested to be effective only if underpinned by values and actions that maintain it. At the level of national and international organisations, the idea of diversity mainstreaming goes beyond ensuring equal opportunities to make the monitoring of diversity an inherent aspect of policy and practice. Practicalities in relation to mainstreaming that are mentioned in EU guidance (European Union, 2003) include ensuring that responsibility for writing gender (or diversity) into policy and practice is fully and widely taken, training for awareness is in place and that there is monitoring of the policy and collection of relevant data. The OECD (2004) similarly stresses equal opportunities for men and women, support for equal opportunities policies at all levels, availability of resources, awareness raising and the taking of responsibilities. Such laudable objectives will only be fulfilled where there is sufficient will to ensure that the principles are followed through. If mainstreaming is to be effective, it will deeply affect the culture of the organisation and this will only be possible through the modelling of the leaders and, as indicated above, will also require that sufficient time and money are allocated.

Once organisational policies including mainstreaming are established, their maintenance requires the establishment of targets and their monitoring. Monitoring of targets is more meaningful for large organisations, and not necessarily appropriate in a small school, for example. An illustration of target setting is that the British Civil Service has adopted a 10-Point Plan for 'Delivering a Diverse Civil Service' (Cabinet Office, 2005). The first of the points is the identification of targets for the senior civil service as a whole and for each of the departments. These include that by 2008:

- 37 per cent of the Senior Civil Service should be women;
- 30 per cent of the top management posts should be filled by women;
- 4 per cent of the Senior Civil Service should be from minority ethnic back-grounds;
- 3.2 per cent of the Senior Civil Service should be people with disabilities.

These targets are underpinned by the publication of relevant data every 6 months, the appointment of Civil Service Diversity Champions to monitor progress on the plan and to meet quarterly and report annually, while departmental champions will report every six months. The most senior civil servants, the Permanent Secretaries, are accountable for diversity in their Departments and Agencies. The identification of hard targets, the fixing of clear target dates and ensuring that lines of account-ability are clear are all mooted as essential to the implementation of a policy that goes beyond rhetoric.

Despite these developments, monitoring is not necessarily clear and simple. In the varied higher education sector of England, HEFCE (2004, p. 8) gives guidance for benchmarking recruitment that varies according to the nature of the post. This means that: 'the representation of women, ethnic minorities, disabled people and people of certain religions in, say, the local community, might provide the statisti-cal record against which the HEI would benchmark its data for locally recruited staff, who will probably be in support roles'. However, comparative data will be dif-ferent for academic staff who are likely to be drawn from a national or even inter-national pool. In Northern Ireland, there is a statutory requirement to monitor for religion and the University of Ulster therefore defines the catchment area for each type of job on each of its four campuses to ensure that the appropriate comparators for monitoring the religion of candidates are in place.

There are further subtleties in monitoring different aspects of diversity. A case study at the University of Newcastle upon Tyne (HEFCE, 2004, p. 21) showed that staff did not always declare disability when it might be appropriate to do so. A sur-vey of staff to raise awareness of disability, and some briefing sessions which included the announcement of the appointment of an adviser for disabled staff meant that there was enhanced understanding of disability and that more staff were identified for support.

Whilst it is now relatively straightforward and accepted in the UK that staff may be classified for monitoring purposes, particularly on the established equal oppor-tunities issues of sex, ethnicity or disability, there is greater uncertainty about how to monitor the potentially more sensitive areas like sexual orientation or religion and probably a greater reluctance to reveal information on the part of the individ-ual. Age is another area where there is uncertainty at present due to the fact that age has been relatively recently included in the UK legislation on discrimination.

The macro level is therefore the frameworks – political, legal and institutional – within which the educational leader operates, but the micro level is the values of the individual and the resulting stance that they might take in relation to diversity.

The individual as leader

Discussing leadership, feminism and social justice, Blackmore (2006, p. 196) states:

> The issue is not the distinction between leadership and management, as good leadership is reliant upon effective management, but between critical and non-critical approaches to leadership, i.e., those who explicitly argue an agenda for social justice. If school leaders and teachers are not prepared to lead to reduce inequality, who will?

Chapter 6 discussed in some detail the emergence of critical approaches to leadership, and particularly the work of Begley and Woods. As Begley (2003) points out, literature on leadership and management has largely been concerned with the organisational perspective and has paid relatively little regard to the values that are held by individuals in leadership roles. As suggested throughout the book, leaders in education may find that analysing the values that they hold is helpful as a starting point. For example, Begley talks about the importance of consequences, self-interest and ethics/principles in terms of motivation. Begley's analysis starts to show the way in which the individual leader can analyse their motivations and attitudes and those of others. Such an 'audit' may be necessary to help reach the state of 'mindfulness' (Gudykunst, 1995, p. 16), which involves attempting to overcome unconscious prejudice that relies on broad stereotypes and classifications and aiming to give attention to the multiplicity of distinctions between individuals (see Chapter 7). This concept provides a foundation not only for the practice of the individual leader, but also for the ways in which she or he may influence those around them to operate. The concept of mindfulness could infuse and underpin the culture of an institution. Leadership is particularly important in relation to diversity because the views and values held by leaders will imbue the culture of the organisation, setting the tone as inclusive and respectful of others, enabling staff to contribute to discussion and decision making and to feel competent and supported in their daily work as well as in their career progress. Looking beyond schools and other educational organisations to small and medium-sized commercial companies, Schminke et al. (2005) have undertaken empirical work that shows a relationship between the leaders' moral development and employee attitudes. The relationship is clearly identified, but it is moderated by two factors: the consistency of the leader's attitudes with their actions and by the age of the organisation. It is not surprising that the younger organisations are more likely to be responsive to the attitudes of the leader at a time when the values and vision of an organisation are still in development, but the importance of setting the culture remains. It is also to be expected that the more that consistency is shown by leaders the more likely it is that their attitudes will impact on staff. The foundation of organisational change in the personal change of each leader is discussed further in Chapter 9.

Leadership and institutional culture

There is an important reciprocal relationship between the leader of an organisation and the culture of that organisation. This has been recognised particularly in the field of school improvement (Hargreaves, 1995; Hopkins, 1994). The culture of an organisation is particularly relevant to the way in which diversity issues are handled. Stone and Colella (1996) identify a number of ways in which the management and leadership impact on the culture in relation to employees with disabilities, but they could easily be applicable to a wider concept of diversity. They identify the types of values that are likely to impede or support the employment of disabled (or other potentially disadvantaged) employees.

> In particular we believe that the values associated with competitive achievement, rugged individualism, self-reliance, in-group superiority, or conformity in appearance may negatively affect the degree to which disabled individuals are viewed as qualified for jobs. However, when organizations value social justice, egalitarianism, and engender norms of cooperation and helpfulness, disabled individuals should be viewed as more suitable for jobs and more capable of making contributions to the organization. (Stone and Colella, 1996, p. 373)

It is clear that a leader will have a role in establishing and modelling these values and that in so doing will affect the culture of the organisation.

An initial step that is both practical and symbolic may be to ensure that there is a formal policy on equality/diversity in the institution (Coleman, 2002). In Chapter 3, one of the ten case study colleges, the only one where real efforts had been made to be inclusive, was discussed (see pp. 38–40). Amongst the measures adopted were an equality action plan and codes of practice for the behaviour of staff and students towards each other.

Hallinger and Heck (2003) conducted an examination of the link between school improvement and leadership and came to the conclusion that leadership is particularly important in three areas: establishing the purpose (vision, mission and goals) of the institution; establishing structures and social networks that foster collaboration; and being people-oriented in what they do. All three of these aspects of the culture can be imbued with consideration and valuing of diversity. This can be seen in policy and mission statements, in HRM practices, but also in the more subtle ways in which messages are put across. It is easy for minority ethnic members of staff to be sidelined into working with other minority ethnic staff or students, and important that structurally they are included in senior management teams to give positive messages to others about inclusion and capabilities. It is important that all staff have opportunities to take on the short-term projects that give them valuable experience and credibility as knowledgeable managers. There are many practical steps that leaders can take to enhance the establishment of a culture that is positive for diversity and values the range of experience and background that all staff can bring.

Staff training and development

Organisational action for promoting diversity and social justice goes beyond the establishment of a policy. Although respect for diversity can be inculcated through all aspects of human resource management, a direct approach is to involve staff in training that relates specifically to diversity. The case study college in Chapter 3 ran frequent development events in relation to specific aspects of diversity, had universal staff entitlement to development opportunities and ran supportive networks e.g. the Black Managers Network. The subtleties of monitoring (see above) are such that there may be a call for development and training of those individuals in human resource management who are responsible for tracking and for maintenance of data bases.

Although they remain sceptical about training for diversity, Stone and Colella (1996) suggest programmes that expose stereotypes about disability, showing their inaccuracy, give clear information about how to treat disabled people and also work to decrease the anxiety that may be felt by those working alongside disabled people. They also suggest that the successes of disabled employees are publicised. These examples are related to disability but exposing stereotypes and increasing knowledge through training are relevant to all aspects of diversity. One problem with diversity training is that it may expose those who do not meet the white, male, able-bodied norms and may actually have the potential of exacerbating problems. Writing about the experience of black women attending workshops for their career development, Crawley (2006, p. 175) comments:

> Workshop participants who had been required to attend organisational diversity training talked about feeling both isolated and 'picked on' at the same time. Their isolation was usually physical in that only one or two of them were likely to be represented within a specific training group. They felt 'picked on' because of the constant pressure to provide a 'black perspective' to the discussions.

Development for members of minority groups can be incorporated into the practice of setting and monitoring targets. At Leeds Metropolitan University monitoring targets to increase the proportion of women and ethnic minority candidates in senior academic posts revealed that they were meeting with a lack of success at the interview stage. As a result those women and BME candidates who had been short-listed, but who were not successful at the interview, were encouraged to join development programmes and to form support networks and mentoring sets. As a result, women in senior posts nearly reached the 35 per cent target, and the percentage of ethnic minority staff in senior roles increased to 2 per cent (HEFCE, 2004).

About half the women secondary head teachers in England offered specific career development for women teachers (Coleman, 2005a). This included their being given the management of short-term projects, attending women-only courses and mentoring. Many of the women secondary heads had undertaken one-to-one interviews with all their staff, ensuring that they gave the necessary encouragement to staff for them to see that they were capable of a successful application for promotion.

Mentoring and role models

Potentially, there is a special place for mentoring and the use of role models in the development of members of disadvantaged groups (Coleman, 2002). Women head teachers (Coleman, 2005b) had felt particularly supported by their previous head teachers, even more than by their families, but mentoring had been experienced by only about 60 per cent of all except the youngest age groups. The higher percentage of the youngest group was probably due to the recent introduction of the compulsory NPQH programme which includes a mentoring element. Mentoring and role models for BME leaders has been discussed in Chapter 5. However, having a mentor and benefiting from one are two different things. Mentoring is plagued by the lack of time normally allocated to it in busy institutions, by insufficient training for mentors and differing expectations of mentors and mentees (Bush et al., 1995). The differing expectations may be due to short-comings of training but may also be associated with matching. There is a debate about whether women should be mentored by women (Kram, 1983) and about sexual harassment entering into a cross-gender mentoring arrangement (Hurley, 1996). There is also a debate about whether aspiring BME leaders should have or would benefit from having white mentors. Obviously the shortage of senior black and or female individuals makes it unlikely that matching can occur as a matter of course and there is also an argument that disadvantaged individuals may actually benefit from being mentored by those who have automatic respect and relative access to power, i.e. white, middle-class males.

The concept of role modelling has also been seen as important in the development of those regarded as disadvantaged. However laudable the idea may be in principle, it can be critiqued as supporting assimilation to ensure that the majority ways of thinking and behaving are taken on board by the aspiring minority group. The black American lawyer Richard Delgado graphically makes the point:

> A white-dominated institution hires you not because you are entitled to or deserve the job. Nor is the institution seeking to set things straight because your ancestors and others of your heritage were systematically excluded from such jobs. Not at all. You're hired (if you speak politely, have a neat haircut, and, above all, can be trusted) not because of your accomplishments, but because of what others think you will do for them. If they hire you now and you are a good role model, things will be better in the next generation. *Footnote to this* (In other words, the next generation of people of color will be like the industrious, well-mannered role model.) (Delgado, 1991, p. 1226)

Some scepticism about the processes of mentoring and role modelling may be salutary, but mentoring remains an important aspect of support for those from diverse backgrounds in accessing leadership roles.

An innovative adaptation of 'reverse' mentoring has been adopted in a commercial sphere (Ian Dodds Consulting, 2006), where the mentor is 'e.g. younger, different gender or ethnicity or sexual orientation' and is coached to have skills to give their leader feedback on the extent to which the leader who aspires to being inclusive is actually practising their intended behaviour. The reverse mentor then makes suggestions of what else the leader should do to be a more effective diversity role model. This provides a double benefit of development both for the senior leader and for the high-potential mentor.

Implications for the training of leaders

The criticism that educational leadership and management marginalise social justice and equity issues is central to this book and noted elsewhere (Osler, 2006).

As mentioned in Chapter 5, the training programmes for all educational leaders both in the USA and in England are unlikely to deal systematically with issues of diversity and social justice (Coleman, 2005a; Rusch, 2004). In fact, most programmes are notable for excluding overt engagement with such issues. In an attempt to remedy this, Capper et al. (2006) have undertaken a review of social justice literature in the USA from which they have extracted a framework for preparing leaders for social justice in education. Such a framework might not be used just in the training of leaders, but could be adapted by them in their own leadership role to extend knowledge and understanding of social justice issues to their staff. The framework identified what is referred to as 'critical consciousness': the examination and identification of the values of the individual, much as mentioned above in the section on fostering change in the individual. The framework also includes knowledge, e.g. of language acquisition, disability and laws relating to special educational needs, practical skills, e.g. of use of data for monitoring, and of hiring and supervising appropriate staff. These three areas are then applied to the curriculum, to pedagogy and to assessment, all with the focus on social justice. What is also a key to the application of the framework is that those preparing for leadership are in an environment and conditions where they 'experience a sense of emotional safety that will help them take risks toward social justice ends' (Capper et al., 2006, p. 212). Much of this framework is devoted to the needs of a diverse student body, but the concepts are also intended to apply to staff and the aspiring leaders are encouraged to conduct equity audits in their own or others' schools. Practical and innovative suggestions for consciousness raising include:

(1) cultural autobiographies;
(2) live histories by interviewing someone older than 65 and who attended school in the USA;
(3) prejudice reduction workshops;
(4) reflective analysis journals that professors respond to and ask critical questions and students analyze;
(5) rational discourse using critical incidents, controversial readings, struc-

tured group activities;

(6) cross cultural interviews;

(7) educational plunges; and

(8) diversity panels.

(Capper et al., 2006, pp. 216–17)

It is clear that some of these suggestions are context-bound, but opening up dialogue with those of a different culture, age and background would seem to be an appropriate aspect of training for leaders in education. An example of an initiative developed at New Mexico State University (McClellan and Dominguez, 2006, p. 234) was a four-day trip along the US/Mexican border for students of educational leadership. This involved their visiting a range of educational institutions on both sides of the border, which would: 'provide for reflective contemplation of the social, economic, and political dilemmas facing traditional education systems', and enable them 'to become more aware of their communities'. However, real life experience can be complemented by more traditional study. Students on the same programme were enthused by the importance of theory in enhancing their understanding of leadership and talked about new material as 'seeping into my everyday life' (p. 234).

Not all efforts at feeding in a social justice element to leadership programmes are so successful. Young and Mountford (2006) report on an attempt to introduce transformational learning around the topic of gender in a year-long course of educational leadership training. Transformational learning here was intended to: 'shift preconceived assumptions and biases about issues related to diversity and subsequently change their [those on the course] leadership behaviors' (p. 266). This initiative therefore was about individual aspiring leaders examining their values and changing them. The outcome over a year was that some thought their beliefs had changed to some extent, but the effects were generally disappointing, with many of the students exhibiting resistance in the same way as that outlined in Chapter 5 (Allard and Santoro, 2006; King, 2004).

In the case of the student leaders exposed to learning about gender, Young and Mountford (2006, p. 268) identified general resistance to engagement with the material. They classify the resistance as either distancing, opposition or intense emotion and this classification may be helpful to leaders who wish to understand and support change of attitudes in their staff.

- Distancing – sexism or racism is believed to be at the level of the individual not the institution, social justice is seen as an issue for others, and not them.
- Opposition – they deny that there is a problem any longer, e.g. state that men and women are completely equal now. They may even 'flip' the issue (p. 268), claiming that it is men who are now oppressed. Alternatively they may say that the issue is just something about which 'the faculty member has an axe to grind'.
- Intense emotions – can include guilt, anger and fear of being seen as a bigot.

The study also revealed that the students felt they had insufficient time to engage with the materials and to discuss them. Capper et al. (2006) refer to the need for emotional space to discuss issues of diversity. There may be a tendency for social justice and diversity issues to be just added on, and/ or crowded out where competition for scarce time and other resources exists.

In summary – implications for leadership

This chapter has provided an overview of actions to promote diversity for and by leaders. A primary tenet of diversity is the appreciation of each individual free of categorisation and stereotyping, using the concept of mindfulness (Gudykunst, 1995). This would seem to be predicated on the examination and possible modification of individual leader values (Begley, 2003) or critical consciousness (Capper et al., 2006). The tenor adopted by the leader will infiltrate the culture of the organisation which can then be bolstered by taking specific action in relation to policy making, monitoring targets, professional development and support, and human resource management. The importance of recognising and valuing diversity and making it central to the organisation has been stressed and it is clear that genuine mainstreaming with the allocation of sufficient time and emotional space is vital. It is, however, unwise to take what has been presented in this chapter as a 'recipe' as if it was uncontested and straightforward. The cognitive and structural difficulties involved in changing deeply held beliefs have been discussed elsewhere in the book. The slippery nature of the language remains a continuing challenge; for example, concepts of equal opportunities and affirmative action are interpreted in ways that are diametrically opposed, diversity as a concept is not always seen as comprehensive and is now often used as a synonym for ethnicity. The challenge of promoting diversity whilst ensuring that individual aspects of diversity such as gender or disability or ethnicity are not overlooked remains. Jones (2006, p. 155) is writing here from the point of view of a black woman, but her questions and conclusion are relevant to all aspects of diversity:

> Is it possible to initiate a diversity policy that not only recognises differences, but at the same time ensures that policies and practices challenge inequality? This seems to me to be the key challenge in managing diversity. The way forward demands critical engagement with the 'intersecting hierarchies of gender, race, economic class, sexuality, religion, disability and age. This acknowledgement of intersectionality and commitment to diversity suggest that a future equality agenda should emphasise equity through difference.

This emphasis on equity can only be achieved through leaders taking action to implement and institutionalise the valuing of difference.

9

Diversity as a positive within leadership

All change

Chapter 7 concluded that in order for diversity issues to be adequately addressed, the attitudes and practice of the dominant group and the structures which it has established require adjustment. Chapter 8 explored policy and development initiatives that might be undertaken as one part of an overall strategy to increase equity. This chapter explores further the kinds of change that may be needed in order to ensure that diversity within educational leadership is a positive.

To date, despite an increasingly diverse workforce, change in the practice of leadership has been relatively minor. 'The staff, one might say, gets diversified but the work does not' (Thomas and Ely, 1996, p. 81). Either change is spasmodic and/or peripheral or has the opposite effect to that intended. Dass and Parker (1999, p. 71) suggest a number of levels of engagement, from resistance, ignoring diversity, seeing diversity as a threat, to a learning perspective that is proactive and strategic in relation to equity issues. The latter level is uncommon. Even when it is achieved, employers who make strenuous efforts to embed equity are confounded by apparently immovable perceptions of unfairness in the organisation. The 'yawning gap' between intention and result persists (Gagnon and Cornelius, 2000, p. 3).

To achieve noticeable change, leading will involve a more stringent and holistic effort, addressing simultaneously the inequities research has uncovered. Educators are, of course, well used to undertaking a sophisticated analysis of disadvantage in relation to learners. The move to personalised learning is in part a recognition of the need to understand fully and take cognisance of the multiple influences on learners which may disadvantage or shape learning. However, leaders do not generally transfer the complexity of their analysis and strategy in relation to diverse learners to leading diverse teams of staff. Strategies here tend to be absent or minimal, concerned mostly with recruiting a diverse profile of team members but with little follow up to achieve equality and inclusion. This is the equivalent of recruiting more diverse students but then assuming one can go on teaching in the same way. The previous chapters have argued that leading within a diverse staff demands considerably more complexity of understanding than we believe is generally the case.

110

A number of overlapping aims have been suggested for leaders in increasingly diverse contexts:

- To instil confidence not just in themselves as leaders but also to build employees' confidence in each other (DiTomaso and Hooijberg, 1996).
- To redistribute power 'beyond a "numbers game"' (Gagnon and Cornelius, 2000, p. 3).
- To attend to the requirements of individuals as well as the organisation (Irby et al., 2002).
- To move beyond notions of sameness and difference, where the latter is measured by a dominant norm (Liff and Wajcman, 1996).

In short, educational leaders will need to change a great deal simultaneously at a variety of levels to have any significant effect. This chapter builds on the previous chapter to explore further how leaders may need to lead change; they may need to change themselves, to change their approaches to teamwork and to change organisational structures, stressing that it is not diversity itself which is a problem requiring attention, but the social and organisational structures and individual orientations which form the context for diversity.

Achieving such a shift is a high priority within education. Effective leadership in diverse contexts is fundamental to the success of schools, colleges and universities. Not only is it necessary to achieve the organisational performance required in the short to medium term, but long term it provides a model of how leadership is practised for learners and the wider community. If schools, colleges and universities cannot successfully model equity and inclusion in leadership, then future generations may take their place in society inadequately equipped as citizens, employees and potential leaders.

Changing oneself

'The personal is political' (Wright Mills, 1959), once a phrase which resonated with a generation, has largely dropped out of common use. It is, however, as useful an indicator of necessary action as it ever was. Recognising the need for change in oneself is not common (Lumby et al., 2005). Many people in education assume the change that is necessary is external only; that it is other people's attitudes or structures or processes which require adjustment. Sometimes change is further distanced in that it is assumed that such things require attention in other organisations, but not one's own. The locus of the problem is removed from the person or the organisation: 'Not a problem here.' There is also a confusion of personal conscious intent with the reality of the lived experience of others. A rebuttal of charges of discrimination, indeed an expressed horror of such, is a common reaction amongst educators and other leaders more widely, when asked to think about their orientation to diversity (Lumby et al., 2005; Smithson and Stokoe, 2005). Leaders assume that because they believe they do not intend discrimination, others do not experience it.

Previous chapters of this book have explored the unconscious cognitive and affective processes which create disadvantage. A number of requirements for change in leadership (both its members and its practice) have emerged. Chapter 3 suggested that the disadvantage experienced by those considered 'other' in education is rarely a result of deliberate and conscious acts of, for example, racism or sexism. Rather, disadvantage results from the usually unconscious creation of 'other' in relation to a norm, and the allocation of inferior status to other. The first step in changing oneself as a leader is therefore the 'mindfulness' discussed in Chapter 7 (Gudykunst, 1995, p. 16); that is, being aware of one's own thought and communication processes and their emotional impact, being aware of other perspectives and being open to new information. A second requirement which follows the insights of mindfulness is to acknowledge that there are issues that demand change, not just generally, but in oneself, one's organisation, department, team. Relentless demands for upbeat public relations make it difficult for school, college and university leaders to acknowledge that disadvantage is a reality in their own organisation, that some colleagues are likely to suffer disadvantage and that this will be challenging to transform. Nevertheless, the validation by leaders of the perspective of those who are disadvantaged is important (Dreaschlin et al., 2000). A third element in the armoury to achieve change is willingness to deal not just with process and structure but with the 'emotion work' referred to in Chapter 3. Anger and resistance, not just in others, but also in oneself, require attention (DiTomaso and Hooijberg, 1996). Finally, Chapter 6 explored the nature of redressing power differentials and disadvantage in relations; such an endeavour is ongoing and will never be fully achieved. The fourth element is therefore willingness to live long term with uncertainly, ambiguity, partial success and partial failure. Such cognitive, affective and behavioural competences have been identified as the components of cultural fluency in research concerning leadership in multinational corporations involving three dimensions, 'cognitive complexity, emotional energy and psychological maturity' (Iles and Kaur Hayers, 1997, p. 105). To summarise, educational leaders who determine to effect change in communities will need all these aspects of competence as a personal and organisational foundation:

- Mindfulness, being aware of one's own thought and communication processes and their impact.
- Acknowledgement of the need for change at personal, individual, group and organisational levels.
- Willingness to deal with emotion work.
- Willingness to live long term with uncertainty, ambiguity, partial success and partial failure.

Changing teamwork

The next level of change is within teams. Teamwork is often seen as a means of improving the cohesion of staff and also improving performance. Maznevski (1994, p. 5) makes two propositions:

PROPOSITION 1. Other things being equal, groups with high integration perform better than groups with low integration on complex decision-making tasks.

PROPOSITION 2. The relationship between diversity and performance is moderated by integration such that: (a) groups with high diversity and high integration perform better than groups with low diversity, but (b) groups with high diversity and low integration perform worse than groups with low diversity.

In other words, diverse teams may improve performance but may also worsen it. How then is leadership to ensure that diverse teams function positively?

Team formation

First, there is a question of how teams are formed and perceived. Gurin and Nagda (2006), writing in relation to students on USA campuses, present social psychological theories which can inform understanding of the way groups and teams are manipulated. They distinguish *decategorisation*, which aims to ensure in-groupers relate to out-group members as individuals rather than as members of a group. The strategy is to personalise relations and thereby avoid the stereotypes attached to out-groups. By contrast, *recategorisation* draws out-group students into the in-group, through common tasks and symbols of identity. Difference is de-emphasised in order to create one single group rather than an in-group and out-groups. A third strategy, *intragroup solidarity*, emphasises differences and supports those groups, which find strength through a shared characteristic (black groups, women-only groups). Such groups may reinterpret as strength what is seen as weakness by in-groups, for example the emotionality of women, black and queer power. The intention is to reduce the powerlessness of out-group members by facilitating their mutual solidarity with other out-group members. Such solidarity lends strength to each other.

Gurin and Nagda (2006) question whether the approaches are mutually exclusive or whether they are able to exist in parallel. They contend that all those things which seek to reduce the boundaries between groups inevitably weaken the solidarity within groups. This may be a reasonable trade-off for the powerful in-group, which has the most power. In-groups can afford to relinquish some strength by assimilating outsiders, thereby reducing solidarity and decreasing the power of out-groups to challenge their norms. However, for the out-groups, weakening boundaries can be destructive of a critical source of strength. Minimising the difference of out-group members may offer them entry to the in-group but at the cost of weakening or severing those ties with the out-group which support self-worth and keep alienation and isolation in bounds.

Teams and identity

We have argued in this volume that renouncing one's own identity by assimilation to an in-group is not a desired outcome. It neither enhances performance nor the individual's rights. Losing the different perspectives and experience of those deemed 'other' negates the very advantages suggested to accrue through diversity. Nor can losing one's identity be seen as a contribution to fairness or equity on an individual basis. As an alternative, Gurin and Nagda (2006, p. 21) propose a 'dual identity model [where] members of groups can be simultaneously attached to their separate group identities and capable of engaging in common tasks with members of other groups'. The key strategy to achieve such dualism is inter-group dialogue where discussion to explore identity, power and interpersonal relations is engineered between different groups of students. This resonates with the strategies to raise critical consciousness discussed in Chapter 8.

What can be learned from this USA experience of addressing diversity amongst students, and how does it relate to leading teams? The suggested aim is to facilitate membership of the in-group for 'outsiders' while they retain membership of an out-group. This is to be achieved by deliberate strategies to foster greater mindfulness of the power flows and cognitive/affective processes that influence relations. Something of this strategy may be transferable to leadership teams, but with caution. Some members of out-groups feel strongly that they wish to retain the identity of their out-group: others do not. Some may primarily wish to be seen as a member of the in-group or of the out-group. Bush et al. (2005, p. 74) found in their survey of black and minority ethnic school leaders that most argued they 'were "leaders" first and "black leaders" second'. In the *Leading Learning* project, one black woman senior leader felt:

> I want to celebrate diversity and act as a role-model, as a black manager and I am comfortable with that, but I also want to be a role model for all people, including a white male team.

In the first case, membership of the in-group was the preferred first identification. In the second case, membership of the out-group was the primary identification, but with the in-group membership also firmly emphasised. Awareness of individuals' membership of groups and the preference of each individual to be defined in single, dual or multiple memberships is part of the necessary mindfulness of leaders. A team is but one group which overlaps potentially with several other groups within the organisation and beyond. Perceiving an individual as a member of the senior leadership team, for example, and defining their role as such may exclude other group memberships which may be of vital importance to the team member, particularly where the other groups are out-groups.

Team functioning

There is very little research on diversity in education teams. What little there is relates generally to a single characteristic: women or black and minority ethnic people in teams. Within the generic literature, the picture that emerges of diverse team functioning is not encouraging. Those who are perceived as other within a team often feel alienated and consequently limit or reserve their contribution (Milliken and Martins, 1996). The habitual response to stress is fight or flight, and therefore, not surprisingly, research indicates greater conflict and turnover amongst diverse teams (Dreaschlin et al., 2000). The causes of conflict are perceived in various ways. For some, conflict may appear to be because of strains associated with role. Role tension, role ambiguity, role overload are seen to be the cause of team dysfunction (Hall, 1997b). For others, it is not role but differences such as ethnicity or gender which are at the heart of conflict and withdrawal. For example, Wallace and Hall (1994) analysed the differences in use of language by men and women which undermine communication amongst senior school teams.

There may be differences in the attribution of team strain and team success:

> Negative behaviour (conflict, delays) by outgroup members may be attributed externally (e.g. provocation). Similarly positive outgroup actions may be attributed externally (luck, ease of task) whereas positive ingroup actions may be attributed internally (effort, ability, etc.). In short, attributions tend to favour the ingroup ... The high performance of women and black people may be attributed by white males to luck or task easiness; that of white males to effort or ability. (Iles and Kaur Hayers, 1997, pp. 108–9)

Differing analyses of why thing are going wrong and why they are going right may lead to multiple and confusing views of how the team is performing and what might require attention in order to improve performance. There is no simple response to such confusion. Logically, a first step would be to surface the differences in order to reach a decision on how team performance might be ameliorated. Communication is not an answer in itself, but it is the foundation of searching for an answer.

Communication

In the sparse research related to diversity and teams, communication emerges as a key factor, defined as 'the successful transmission of meaning as it was intended from each person to the others in the group' (Maznevski, 1994, p. 5). One prerequisite for such successful communication is that debate is allowed. While this sounds obvious, its achievement is far from a common experience. Smith (1997) points out that there is a tendency to punish questioning behaviours or unusual ideas. Mostly this is inadvertent. Argyris' (1991) theories about professionals' learning support this contention. He suggests that professionals are excellent at not learning, at protecting themselves from what is new, and presents four values which consistently shape actions:

1. To remain in control;
2. To maximise 'winning' and minimise 'losing';
3. To suppress negative feelings; and
4. To be as rational as possible – by which people mean defining clear objectives and evaluating their behaviour in terms of whether or not they have achieved them.

(Argyris, 1991, p. 103)

These values display a tendency to protect oneself by avoiding uncertainty, and echo Gudykunst's (1995) depiction of communication as essentially self-protective, as discussed in Chapter 3. Argyris sees well-educated professionals as particularly susceptible to such tendencies. This being the case, those who see things differently, who question actions, processes and particularly goals, may be seen as obstructive or difficult. It is no wonder that those who are seen as other, whose perceptions may differ from those of the dominant group, may feel alienated and limit their contribution within a team.

The fact that stereotyping, discrimination, disadvantage in relation to staff persists in our schools, colleges and universities is embarrassing to educators. As Argyris put it in conversation with Crossman:

As human beings, we embrace truth only when it is not threatening or embarrassing. Otherwise we hide it, or massage it. (Crossman, 2003, p. 42)

The start of the chapter identified acknowledgement of the issues not just in the generality but close to home as a key competence to lead in a diverse society. Stating that debate must be allowed is therefore not the simplistic statement of the obvious that it first appears. Rather it is a profound challenge that will call on the personal skills, confidence and determination of leaders to allow those perspectives and issues to surface which it would be more comfortable to bury.

Listening

If debate is allowed, then mode of listening is a related competence. Leaders may claim that they 'always listen'. However, just as allowing debate is not the simple skill it appears, listening to staff is equally challenging. A foundation skill for leaders is the ability to 'decenter' (Maznevski, 1994, p. 7) rather than to egocentre. The key is not so much to put oneself into another's position socially but to put oneself into their cognitive position. This is extremely challenging for leaders. Rather as with optical illusions, a sustained effort is necessary to hold in one's mind something different to what was first perceived, and any slight shift or lapse of concentration results in swift reversion to default mode of understanding. Additionally, there may be little desire to achieve such a shift in perspective as habitual perspectives, unconsciously learned over time, appear 'right' and 'natural' (Allix and Gronn, 2005). This epistemological bias may result in another perspective appearing simply 'wrong' and attempts to appreciate or tolerate it may be painful and feel morally questionable. How then to navigate amongst competing perspectives and preferences for action? Maznevski (1994, p. 8) suggests that a move from an implicit process of negotiation to explicit agreements may be helpful in diverse teams:

> There must be some agreement among participants about how the interaction will take place ... Norms of participation, selection of a leader, conflict management mechanisms, and so on must all be agreed upon. This negotiation endorsement process often takes place implicitly. Participants enter a group equipped with a repertoire of norms learned in similar situations. If this repertoire is common to all members, the negotiation process is simple and virtually automatic. ... if the norms are not similar and a common set of norms is not explicitly negotiated, then achieving effective communication is unlikely.

Agreeing how the team is to communicate, how it is to deal with differences in perceptions, goals and ways of achieving them, is uncommon in education. Communication generally revolves around persuasion, and the power base of the individual speaking influences their persuasiveness. Sometimes the coercion of authority is invoked, but often cloaked in consultation, the contrived collegiality identified by Hargreaves (1992), which leads to false consensus as discussed in Chapter 6. As an alternative to persuasion or coercion, Prasad and Mills (1997, p. 65) distinguish *toleration*, which implies 'putting up' with others, and *appreciation*:

> where people *not only allow or even adapt some behaviours of people from other cultures, they integrate some of them into their being* ... where people are not merely trying to manage diversity and conform it to corporate or individual goals; instead they are attempting to incorporate valuable aspects of the different groups (ethnic, religious, political and so on) to enhance themselves and the organizations to which they belong. (p. 65; emphasis in the original)

Agreeing processes of communication and cultivating appreciation rather than tolerance is therefore a possible strategy to achieve integration.

Integration

Both Maznevski and ourselves have used the term integration without considering its meaning in detail. The term is often used as shorthand to indicate the aim of diverse team working. Ethnographic material on the experience of working within a diverse education team is sparse. We are generally driven back to imagination and empathy to understand how those who are perceived as other experience teamwork. Some insight is gained by examining the work Reynolds and Trehan undertook in relation to a leadership preparation programme. Their analysis of how the group integrated or not is based on interviews with participants. They discovered differences in the experience of the programme related to:

- professional, social or academic background;
- ways of working together;
- structural differences (gender, age);
- public–private boundaries.

(Reynolds and Trehan, 2003, p. 168)

The critique drawn from their data echoes the discussion about leadership theory in Chapter 6 of this volume. The leadership programme offered little opportunity to foreground difference. Those within the group who were perceived or perceived themselves as other felt distanced and faced a choice of conforming or being marginalised. On the surface this class may well have appeared 'integrated', in that there was no overt conflict. However, what appeared a democratic learning community concealed exclusion. While issues of 'coercion, conformity, deviance, conflict resolution' (2003, p. 165) are in the literature and often formally part of the leadership curriculum, they are dealt with 'stripped of social significance' (p. 165). Conformity, for example, is covered in relation to a generalised staff. Issues such as gender, race and religion are not explicitly linked to conformity. And yet leaders/team members may have different perceptions of leadership and its aims (Shah, 2006b). Such differences remain obscured by silence. The reality within the group in question was buried. Some students were angry. For example, in the words of two programme participants:

> Some of the male members of the group ... seemed intent on literally drowning out others' opinions. It was therefore difficult to get heard unless one adopted some masculine characteristics.

> The two mature members in particular, one male, one female, were particularly dominant, using the power of perceived experience to influence members. (Reynolds and Trehan, 2003, p. 170)

Different ways of working also caused distance. One participant was upset that his preferred silence resulted in a label of 'non-participator'. However, the perspectives of individual angry or upset students were not communicated to the group.

While this was not an education team in a school or college, it does provide a parallel example. This was a group of leaders where what appears to be a community or a group which has democratic processes open to all, in fact privileges some through 'false notions of consensus' (2003, p. 167). Integration cannot imply consensus about goals or ways of working if it is to be inclusive. Nevertheless, decisions are still needed on how to act. An accommodation of difference is achieved if agreement on action is framed by explicit acknowledgement of who is advantaged by the decision. An integrated diverse team would therefore be one where differences and accommodations are openly acknowledged, within a framework of appreciation.

Changing organisational structure and process

The chapter has so far drawn on social psychology to suggest that attitudinal and behavioural change is needed to achieve greater equity in leadership. However, a reliance solely on psychological change would be an incomplete strategy (Reynolds and Trehan, 2003). DiTomaso and Hooijberg (1996) suggest that structures of difference equate to structures of inequality. Structure is the ordering of physical and symbolic elements of resource and experience into persistent patterns. There are, of course, numerous patterns within an educational organisation. The organisation of roles, usually into a hierarchy, is one such ordering. The structure of career and rewards is another. The process by which decisions are reached is a further example.

Norte's (1999) study of the processes of effective school leadership for diversity in 21 school communities in California resulted in a framework for addressing structural issues:

1 Content: the subject matter of focus.
2 Process: how people engage the subject matter.
3 Structure: how time, space and people are organised and configured.
4 Staffing: the roles to which personnel are assigned.
5 Infrastructure: the physical setting.

While 'structure' is designated as one element only, we would argue that within the broad definition of structure we have provided, all of the five elements equate to structures of difference and potentially, inequity.

Content concerns the vision of the leaders which not only states the commitment to inclusion in strategic policies, but ensures such commitment is embedded in all aspects of policy, documents (such as promotional materials) and images. This is the ontological aspect of structure within leadership.

Process relates to how the commitment is enacted. Engagement with staff and the wider community aims to achieve inclusive decision making. There is a large literature taking a micropolitcal perspective on leadership and management, examining the power flows and inclusion/exclusion of decision making (Ball, 1987; Becher and Kogan, 1992; Bush, 1995; Hoyle, 1986; Morgan, 1986). However, as discussed in Chapter 2 and above in this chapter, such literature does not generally relate to diversity. While it identifies that individuals and groups may be excluded from power and decision, the excluded are on the whole homogenised abstractions. There is also a literature on managerialism, which suggests that power has been ever more firmly entrenched in senior, largely white male 'top teams' by new public sector management. Simkins (2000) analyses the advent of managerialism in both schools and colleges. Managerialist practice is suggested to be focused on finance, accountability and the 'manager's right to manage' (Elliott and Crossley, 1997; Randle and Brady, 1997). Leonard (1998, p. 78) analyses changes in further education since incorporation in 1993 and notes decisions 'made behind closed doors'. In such an environment, inclusive decision making is very challenging.

'Process' is not a false democratic consensus, but a difficult and sometimes painful path to accommodation and appreciation. It recognises that there is unlikely to be a 'common good' except in the most general of terms. Once discussion moves beyond aspirational aims and actions must be decided, then advantage and disadvantage become the warp and weft of deliberations if inclusion is to be a reality. Process is the structure of inclusion or exclusion in reaching knowledge; it is the epistemological element of structure within leadership.

Structure is how people are shaped into groups and teams. It relates to Gurin and Nagda's (2006) ideas on group formation. How are groups and teams and contact between them to be constituted both within staff and between staff and the wider community? Are decategorisation, recategorisation or intragroup solidarity to be sole or parallel strategies and how are they to be achieved? The nature of diversity amongst the staff and the community and their wishes may influence the decision on strategy. Structure uses the facilitation or barring of contact and communication as a means of controlling power flows. It is the micropolitical element of leadership.

Staffing Where staff are placed in an organisation matters. The ghettoising of black or minority ethnic staff, for example, is an instance where the structure of difference equates to a structure of inequality. In the *Leading Learning* project, one college had minority ethnic staff largely teaching English as an additional language or in service support roles. It was attempting to appoint more minority ethnic staff to management roles but mainly through fixed-term projects. The permanent structure remained largely undented. A first line manager commented on the fact that black and disabled staff were clustered at lower levels of the hierarchy:

> It's as if they see that they can employ disabled and black people at the lower end, but actually there's nothing stopping diverse people from being managers – but they don't see that.

Education staff habitually take note of the distribution of roles through their organisation. In the *Leading Learning* project one member of staff in a first line leader focus group noted:

> The senior management has the largest number of black members of staff on there and that's commendable. When I came to this college two years ago one of the first things I noticed was the black members of senior management and to me it was a welcoming sight.

However, other members of staff commented on the all-black teams of cleaners and the dearth of black leaders at middle levels. Gender differential in a hierarchy is also of note. Leonard (1998) comments on the all-white male senior leadership team in her further education college.

The causes of such hierarchical apartheid are very complex. The reason often given by leaders is that insufficient numbers of minority groups or women apply. Such simplistic analysis may well be disingenuous. Understanding the complex interplay of reasons why the dominant group remains senior in the hierarchy will demand careful analysis not only of recruitment and appointment processes but also other structures, for example career and rewards. This chapter cannot cover in detail the impact of the many structures that may disadvantage. For example, career structures are still predominantly those that existed prior to 1950 and reflect the patterns of white male occupation. Reward systems are equally biased (Korac-Kakabadse and Kouzmin, 1999; Sturges, 1999). A one-size-fits-all career and reward structure is but one mechanism by which structures of differences equate to structures of inequality. Leaders will need to consider the full range, for which Norte (1999) provides more detailed guidance. His briefly stated category of 'staffing' places very great challenges on leaders.

Infrastructure demands that the physical environment is accessible, safe and comfortable for all stakeholders, including those with physical disabilities, and inviting to all sections of the community. While issues of access and facilities for those with physical disabilities, or particular dietary and religious needs, are commonly recognised, more subtle issues of space often are not. An analysis of the allocation of space by gender, for example, could be an informative exercise.

Norte's (1999) framework directs leaders to consider the multiple aspects of structure which may be contributing to inequity. While it might be used to frame no more than the ubiquitous initiatives (saying welcome in several languages in the foyer, stating a commitment to equal opportunities on job advertisements etc.), it could also be used to go considerably further in thinking and acting in response.

In summary – framing progress

How then might one frame the underlying approach to leading schools, colleges and universities successfully in a diverse and unequal society? This book has essentially criticised the assumed homogeneity of much educational leadership theory and practice. It has suggested that both are implicated in the maintenance of the status quo, seeing the need for social change as gradual and limited, 'building consensus and social order, often within the boundaries of *existing authoritative and control structures*' (Nemetz and Christensen, 1996, p. 438). We have adopted an alternative radical stance in the light of considerable evidence of the extent of inequity in education. Critical race theory suggests that racism is a permanent reality (Bell, 1995). Radical feminist approaches also stress that patriarchy is not overcome (Acker, 1994; Blackmore, 1999). Many individuals whose characteristics render them 'other' in the eyes of the dominant continue to be excluded, or included only at the cost of assimilation (Osler, 2006). Those leading in perceived highly diverse contexts, often equated with multicultural communities, perceive a pressure towards 'managing' diversity, as if diversity itself were the problem. Those who perceive their organisation to be sited in a relatively stable and homogeneous community may see an orientation to diversity as a peripheral luxury, generally accommodated by minimum compliance with legislative demands and some degree of multiculturalism in the curriculum.

We have argued that inequality and conflict are the permanent context, although these may be covert rather than overt. Resolution of conflict may merely offer advantage to the successful group, disguising beneath the appearance of harmony the resurgence of inequality in a different form to that which preceded the resolution: it does not obliterate disadvantage. Educational leadership will remain open to comfortable fallacious processes of consensus and harmony; alternatively, it has the potential to embrace more radical perspectives which acknowledge the need to navigate conflict and inequity as a permanent state. Blackmore (2006, p. 196) suggests that the choice facing leaders is between 'critical and non-critical approaches'. This final chapter has suggested that changing oneself is the starting point for a greater mindfulness of the challenges and options, and that each leader has the potential to strive for change and to model greater equity through leadership in our schools, colleges and universities.

There are no simple guidelines for action. Normative codes of practice and suggestions for initiatives emanating from legislation-driven advisory bodies have their place, but they are hazardous. They may provide a means of misdirection and displacement, focusing attention on superficial production of pieces of paper which appear to demonstrate progress but in fact have a tenuous relationship to any meaningful change, distracting staff from a more fundamental engagement with inequity (Deem and Morley, 2006). Even more disquieting, they may provide a cloak, disguising an unwillingness to change by presenting the appearance of commitment while limiting action to the socially acceptable minimum.

While ongoing inequity and conflict is acknowledged, we do not suggest a social determinism that precludes the possibility of progress. Leaders can achieve change, if only in that a persistent and consistent attempt to do so is in itself a powerful communication of challenge to inequity. The stance we have suggested of permanent mindfulness, navigating uncomfortable and sometimes painful realities, requires moral energy and moral stamina. Educators have always been motivated by the intrinsic value of a goal. There can be little that offers greater value to an educational community and to wider society than leading for greater equity and inclusion. While the battle for equality may never be fully concluded, educational leaders at all levels of the educational system may be stirred to contribute to moving our society forward by a determined and mindful stance. Returning to the words in the introductory chapter, to our mind, no action is no option.

References

Acker, S. (1994) *Gendered Education*. Buckingham, Open University Press.

Addi-Raccah, A. (2005) Gender, ethnicity and school principalship in Israel: comparing two organizational cultures. *International Journal of Inclusive Education*, Vol. 9, No. 3, pp. 217–239.

Addi-Raccah, A. and Ayalon, H. (2002) Gender inequality in leadership positions of teachers. *British Journal of Sociology of Education*, Vol. 23, No. 2, pp. 157–177.

Adler, S., Laney, J. and Packer, M. (1993) *Managing Women: Feminism and Power in Educational Management*. Buckingham, Open University Press.

Alexander, M.G. and Levin, S. (1998) Theoretical, empirical and practical approaches to intergroup conflict. *Journal of Social Issues*, Vol. 54, No. 4, pp. 629–639.

Allard, A.D. and Santoro, N. (2006) Troubling identities: teacher education students' constructions of class and ethnicity. *Cambridge Journal of Education*, Vol. 36, No. 1, pp. 115–129.

Allix, N. and Gronn, P. (2005) 'Leadership' as knowledge. *Educational Management, Leadership and Administration*, Vol. 33, No. 2, pp. 181–196.

Archibong, U. (2005) Cultural understanding in leadership and management. *Leadership Foundation Fellowships Programme*, London, 7 November.

Arendt, H. (1972) *Crises of the Republic: Lying in Politics, Civil Disobedience on Violence, Thoughts on Politics and Revolution*. New York, Harcourt Brace Jovanovich.

Argyris, C. (1991) Teaching smart people how to learn. *Harvard Business Review*, May–June, pp. 99–109.

Baldwin, J. and Hecht, M. (1995) The layered perspective of cultural (in)tolerance(s). In R. Wiseman (ed.), *International Communication Theory, Volume XIX*. London, Sage.

Ball, S. (1987) *The Micro-Politics of the School*. London, Routledge.

Becher, T. and Kogan, M. (1992) *Process and Structure in Higher Education*, 2nd edn. Routledge, London.

Begley, P. (2003) In pursuit of authentic school leadership practices. In P. Begley and O. Johansson (eds), *The Ethical Dimensions of School Leadership*. London, Kluwer Academic.

Begley, P. (2004) Understanding valuation processes: exploring the linkage between motivation and action. *International Studies in Educational Administration*, Vol. 32, No. 2, pp. 4–17.

Begley, P.T. (1994) *School Leadership: A Profile Document*, accessed online at www.oise.utoronto.ca/-vsvede, 3 April 2006.

Bell, D. (1995) Racial realism after we're gone: prudent speculations on America in a post-racial epoch. In R. Delgado (ed.), *Critical Race Theory: The Cutting Edge*. Philadelphia, PA, Temple University, pp. 2–8.

Benhabib, S. (2002) *The Claims of Culture: Equality and Diversity in the Global Era*. Princeton, NJ, Princeton University Press.

Bennett, N., Wise, C., Woods, P. and Harvey, J. A. (2003) *Distributed Leadership*. Nottingham, NCSL.

Bhavnani, R. (1994) *Black Women in the Labour Market – A Research Review*. Manchester, Equal Opportunities Commission, quoted in Davidson, M.J. (1997) *The Black and Ethnic Minority Woman Manager: Cracking the Concrete Ceiling*. London, Paul Chapman.

Blackmore, J. (1989) Educational leadership: a feminist critique and reconstruction. In B. Limerick and B. Lingard (eds), *Critical Perspectives on Educational Leadership*. Deakin Studies in Education, Series 2. Lewes, Falmer Press.

Blackmore, J. (1999) *Troubling Women: Feminism, Leadership and Educational Change*. Buckingham, Open University Press.

Blackmore, J. (2004) Leading as emotional management work in high risk times: the counterintuitive impulses of performativity and passion. *School Leadership and Management*, Vol. 24, Issue 4, pp. 439–459.

Blackmore, J. (2006) Social justice and the study and practice of leadership in education: a feminist history. *Journal of Educational Administration and History*, Vol. 38, No. 2, pp. 185–200.

Blair, M. (2002) Effective school leadership: the multi-ethnic context. *British Journal of Sociology of Education*, Vol. 23, No. 2, pp. 179–191.

Bokina, J. (1996) Radical feminism in Canada. *Telos*, Issue 109, pp. 177–182.

Bonnett, A. and Carrington, B. (1996) Constructions of an anti-racist education in Britain and Canada. *Comparative Education*, Vol. 32, No. 3, pp. 271–288.

Boris, E. (1998) Fair employment and the origins of affirmative action in the 1940s. *NWSA Journal*, Vol. 10, Issue 3, pp. 142–151.

Boscardin, M. and Jacobson, S. (1996) The inclusive school: integrating diversity and solidarity through community-based management. *Journal of Educational Administration*, Vol. 35, No. 5, pp. 466–476.

Bowe, R., Ball, S. and Gewirtz, S. (1994) Parental choice, consumption and social theory: the operation of micro markets in education. *British Journal of Educational Studies*, Vol. 42, No. 1, pp. 38–52.

Brooker, L. and Ha, S.J. (2005) The cooking teacher: investigating gender stereotypes in a Korean kindergarten. *Early Years*, Vol. 25, No. 1, pp. 17–30.

Brown, J. and Mitchell B. (2000) Landscape stewardship: new directions in conservation of nature and culture. *The George Wright Forum,* Vol. 17, No. 1, pp. 70–79, accessed online at www.georgewright.org/171brown.pdf, 22 May 2006.

Brunner, C. (2000) *Principles of Power: Woman Superintendents and the Riddle of the Heart.* Albany, NY, State University of New York Press.

Brunner, C. (2002) Professing educational leadership: conceptions of power. *Journal of School Leadership,* Vol. 12, No. 2, pp. 693–720.

Bryant, M. (1998) Cross cultural understandings of leadership: themes from Native American interviews. *Educational Management and Administration,* Vol. 26, No. 1, pp. 7–20.

Bush, T. (1995) *Theories of Educational Management,* 2nd edn. London, Paul Chapman.

Bush, T. and Glover, D. (2003) *School Leadership: Concepts and Evidence.* Nottingham, NCSL.

Bush, T., Coleman, M., Wall, D. and West-Burnham, J. (1995) Mentoring and continuing professional development. In D. McIntyre and H. Hagger (eds), *Mentors in Schools: Developing the Profession of Teaching.* London, David Fulton.

Bush, T., Glover, D. and Sood, K. (2006) Black and minority ethnic leaders in England: a portrait. *School Leadership and Management,* Vol. 26, No. 3, pp. 289–305.

Bush, T., Glover, D., Sood, K., Cardno, C., Moloi, K., Potgeiter, G. and Tangie, K. (2005) *Black and Minority Ethnic Leaders,* Final Report to the National College for School Leadership, Lincoln, International Institute for Education Leadership.

Cabinet Office (2005) *Delivering a Diverse Civil Service: A 10-Point Plan.* London, accessed online at www.diversity-whatworks.gov.uk, 12 June 2005.

Cameron, C. (2001) Promise or problem? A review of the literature on men working in early childhood services. *Gender Work and Organization,* Vol. 8, No. 4 (Oct.), pp. 430–453.

Capper, C., Theoharis, G. and Sebastian, J. (2006) Toward a framework for preparing leaders for social justice. *Journal of Educational Administration,* Vol. 44, No. 3, pp. 209–224.

Chan Kit-wa, Anita (2004) Gender, school management and educational reforms: a case study of a primary school in Hong Kong. *Gender and Education,* Vol. 16, No. 4, pp. 491–510.

Chang, Y., Church, R. and Zikic, J. (2004) Organizational Culture, group diversity and intra-group conflict. *Team Performance Management,* Vol. 10, No. 1/2, pp. 26–34.

Chisholm, L. (2001) Gender and leadership in South African educational administration. *Gender and Education,* Vol. 13, No. 4, pp. 387–399.

Cochrane-Smith, M. (1995) Color blindness and basket making are not the answers: confronting the dilemmas of race, culture, and language diversity in teacher education. *American Educational Research Journal,* Vol. 32, No. 3. pp. 493–522.

Coleman, M. (1994) Leadership in educational management. In T. Bush and J. West-Burnham (eds), *The Principles of Educational Management.* Harlow, Longman.

Coleman, M. (1996a) Management style of female head teachers. *Educational*

Management and Administration, Vol. 24, No. 2, pp. 163–174.

Coleman, M. (1996b) Barriers to career progress for women in education: the perceptions of female head teachers. *Educational Research*, Vol. 38, No. 3, pp. 317–332.

Coleman, M. (2002) *Women as Head Teachers: Striking the Balance*. Stoke-on-Trent, Trentham Books.

Coleman, M. (2004) *Evaluation of the SHINE Programme*. London, London Leadership Centre.

Coleman, M. (2005a) *Gender and Headship in the Twenty-First Century*. Nottingham, NCSL, accessed www.ncsl.org.uk/mediastore/image2/twlf-gender-full.pdf, 5 July 2006.

Coleman, M. (2005b) Women and leadership: the views of women who are 'Leading from the Middle'. Paper presented at the BELMAS conference, Milton Keynes, 23 September.

Collard, J. and Reynolds, C. (2005) *Leadership, Gender and Culture in Education*. Maidenhead, Open University Press.

Crawley, R. (2006) Diversity and the marginalisation of black women's issues. *Policy Futures in Education*, Vol. 4, No. 2, pp. 172–184.

Crompton, R., Brockmann, M. and Wiggin, R.D. (2003) A woman's place ... employment and family life for men and women. In A. Park, J. Curtice, K. Thomson, L. Jarvis and C. Bromley (eds), *British Social Attitudes: The 20th Report. Continuity and Change over Two Decades*. London, Sage.

Crossman, M. (2003) Altering theories of learning and action: an interview with Chris Argyris. *Academy of Management Executive*, Vol. 17, No. 2, pp. 40–46.

Cruikshank, K. (2004) Towards diversity in teacher education: teacher preparation of immigrant teachers. *International Journal of Teacher Education*, Vol. 27, No. 2, pp. 125–138.

Cushman, P. (2005) It's just not a real bloke's job: male teachers in the primary school. *Asia-Pacific Journal of Teacher Education*, Vol. 33, No. 3, pp. 321–338.

Darden, C. (2003) Delivering on diversity leadership: a walk in the other guy's shoes. *Executive Speeches*, June/July 2003, pp. 20–25.

Dass, P. and Parker, B. (1999) Strategies for managing human resource diversity: from resistance to learning. *Academy of Management Executive*, Vol. 13, No. 2, pp. 68–80.

Davidson, M. (1997) *The Black and Ethnic Minority Woman Manager: Cracking the Concrete Ceiling*. London, Paul Chapman.

Davies, L. (1990) *Equity and Efficiency? School Management in an International Context*. London, Falmer Press.

Davies, L. (1998) Democratic practice, gender and school management. In P. Drake and P. Owen (eds), *Gender and Management in Education*. Stoke-on-Trent, Trentham Books.

Day, C., Harris, A., Hadfield, M., Tolley, H. and Beresford, J. (2000) *Leading Schools in Times of Change*. Buckingham, Open University Press.

Decuir, J. and Dixson, A. (2004) 'So when it comes out, they aren't that surprised that it is there': using critical race theory, a tool of analysis of race and racism in education', *Educational Researcher*, Vol. 33, No. 5, pp. 26–31.

Deem, R. and Morley, L. (2006) Diversity in the Academy? Staff perceptions of equality policies in six contemporary higher education institutions. *Policy Futures in Education*, Vol. 4, No. 2, pp.185–202.

Delgado, R. (1991) Affirmative action as a majoritarian device: or, Do you really want to be a role model? *Michigan Law Review*, Vol. 89, No. 5, pp. 1222–1231.

Delgado, R. and Stefancic, J. (2001) *Critical Race Theory: An Introduction.* New York, New York University.

DfES (2004, 2005) *Statistics of Education: School Workforce in England.* www.dfes.gov.uk/rsgateway/DB/VO:?v000380/index.shtml.

Dimmock, C. and Walker, A. (2005) *Educational Leadership: Culture and Diversity.* London, Sage.

DiTomaso, N. and Hooijberg, R. (1996) Diversity and the demands of leadership. *The Leadership Quarterly*, Vol. 7, No. 2, pp. 163–187.

Donohue, W.A. and Kolt, R. (1992) *Managing Interpersonal Conflict.* Newbury Park, CA, Sage.

Dreachslin, J.L., Hunt, P.L. and Sprainer, E. (2000) Workforce diversity: implications for the effectiveness of health care delivery teams. *Social Science and Medicine*, Vol. 50, pp. 1403–1414.

Drucker, P. (1997) Foreword. In F. Hesselbein (ed.), *The Leader of the Future: New Visions, Strategies and Practices for the Next Era* (The Drucker Foundation). San Francisco, CA, Jossey-Bass/Wiley.

Druckman, D. (1994) Determinants of compromising behaviour in negotiation. *Journal of Conflict Resolution*, Vol. 38, No. 3, pp. 507–556.

Elliott, G. and Crossley, M. (1997) Contested values in further education. Findings from a case study of the management of change. *Educational Management and Administration*, Vol. 25, No. 1, pp. 79–92.

Elliott, G. and Hall, V. (1994) FE Inc. – business orientation in further education and the introduction of human resource management. *School Organisation*, Vol. 14, No. 1, pp. 3–10.

Elmore, R. (2000) *Building a New Structure for School Leadership.* Washington, DC, The Albert Shanker Institute.

European Union (2003) Gender Mainstreaming Briefing, accessed online at http://europa.eu.int/comm/employment_social/equ_opp/gms_en.html

Evetts, J. (1994) *Becoming a Secondary Headteacher.* London, Cassell.

Fennell, H.A. (2005) Living leadership in an era of change. *International Journal of Leadership in Education*, Vol. 8, No. 2, pp. 145–165.

Foskett, N. and Lumby, J. (2003) *Leading and Managing Education: International Dimensions.* London, Paul Chapman.

Foti, R.J. and Miner, J.B. (2003) Individual differences and organizational forms in the leadership process. *The Leadership Quarterly*, Vol. 14, pp. 83–112.

Foucault, M. (1980) *Power/Knowledge: Selected Interviews and Other Writings*. Brighton, Harvester.

Fraser, N. (1994) Rethinking the public sphere: a contribution to the critique of actually existing democracy. In H.A. Giroux and P. McLaren (eds), *Between Borders: Pedagogy and the Politics of Cultural Studies*. New York, Routledge.

Fullan, M. (1992) *The Moral Imperative of School Leadership*. London, Sage.

Gagnon, S. and Cornelius, N. (2000) Re-examining workplace equality: the capabilities approach. *Human Resource Management Journal*, Vol. 10, No. 4, pp. 68–87.

Gaine, C. (2001) Promoting equality and equal opportunities: school policies. In D. Hill and M. Cole (eds), *Schooling and Equality. Fact, Concept, and Policy*. London, Kogan Page.

Gantt, E. and Reber, J. (1999) Sociobiological and social constructionist accounts of altruism: a Phenomenological Critique. *Journal of Phenomenological Psychology*, Vol. 30, No. 2, pp. 1–16, accessed online at http://web19.epnet.com/, 4 March 2005.

Gaskell, J. and Taylor, S. (2003) The Women's Movement in Canadian and Australian education: from liberation and sexism to boys and social justice. *Gender and Education*, Vol. 15, No. 2, pp. 151–168.

Gillborn, D. (2004) Anti-racism: from policy to praxis. In G. Ladson-Billings and D. Gillborn (eds), *The RoutledgeFalmer Reader in Multicultural Education*. Abingdon, RoutledgeFalmer.

Gillborn, D. (2005) Education policy as an act of white supremacy: whiteness, critical race theory and education reform. *Journal of Education Policy*, Vol. 20, No. 4, pp. 485–505.

Giddens, A. (1994) *Beyond Left and Right. The Future of Radical Politics*. Cambridge, Polity Press.

Gilligan, G. (1982) *In a Different Voice: Psychological Theory and Women's Development*. Cambridge, MA, Harvard University Press.

Gleeson, D. (2001) Style and substance in education leadership: further education as a case in point. *Journal of Education Policy*, Vol. 16, No. 3, pp. 181–196.

Gleeson, D. and Shain, F. (1999) Managing ambiguity: between markets and managerialism – a case study of 'middle' managers in further education. *The Sociological Review*, Vol. 47, No. 3, pp. 461–490.

Gold, A. (1993) Women friendly management development programmes. In J. Ouston (ed.), *Women in Education Management*. Harlow, Longman.

Gold, A., Evans, J., Earley, P., Halpin, D. and Collarbone, P. (2003) Principled Principals? Values-Driven Leadership: Evidence from Ten Case Studies of 'Outstanding' School Leaders. *Educational Management, Leadership and Administration*, Vol. 31, No. 2, pp. 127–138.

Goldring, E. and Chen, M. (1994) The feminization of the principalship in Israel: the trade-off between political power and cooperative leadership. In C. Marshall (ed.), *The New Politics of Race and Gender*. London, Falmer.

Gorard, S., Fitz, J. and Taylor, C. (2003) *Schools, Markets and Choice Policies*. London,

RoutledgeFalmer.

Gosetti, P. and Rusch, E. (1995) Reexamining educational leadership: challenging assumptions. In D.M. Dunlap and P.A. Schmuck (eds), *Women Leading in Education*. Albany, NY, State University of New York.

Griffiths, M. (2003) *Action for Social Justice in Education: Fairly Different*. Maidenhead, Open University Press.

Grogan, M. (1996) *Voices of Women Aspiring to the Superintendency*. Albany, NY, State University of New York.

Grogan, M. (1999) Equity/equality issues of gender, race and class. *Educational Administration Quarterly*, Vol. 35, No. 4, pp. 518–536.

Grogan, M. (2004) US Women Top Executive Leaders in Education: Building Communities of Learners. Paper presented at the CCEAM Conference, Shanghai, October.

Gronn, P. (2000) Distributed properties: a new architecture for leadership. Paper presented to BEMAS Research 2000, *Leading Educational Management in Learning Societies: Research, Policy and Practice*, The 6th International Educational Management and Administration Research Conference, 29–31 March 2000, Robinson College, Cambridge.

Gronn, P. (2001) Commentary. Crossing the Great Divides: problems of cultural diffusion for leadership in education. *International Journal for Leadership in Education*, Vol. 4, No. 4, pp. 401–414.

Gudykunst, W. (1995) Anxiety/uncertainty management (AUM) theory. In R. Wiseman (ed.), *International Communication Theory, Vol. XIX*. London, Sage.

Gurin, P. and Nagda, B.R.A. (2006) Getting to the what, how and why of diversity on campus. *Educational Researcher*, Vol. 35, No. 1, pp. 20–24.

Hall, V. (1996) *Dancing on the Ceiling: A Study of Women Managers in Education*. London, Paul Chapman.

Hall, V. (1997a) Dusting off the Phoenix: gender and educational management revisited. *Educational Management and Administration*, Vol. 25, No. 3, pp. 309–324.

Hall, V. (1997b) Management roles in education. In T. Bush and D. Middlewood (eds), *Managing People in Education*. London, Paul Chapman.

Hallinger, P. and Heck, R. (2003) Understanding the contribution of leadership to school improvement. In M. Wallace and L. Poulson (eds), *Learning to Lead Critically in Educational Leadership and Management*. London, Sage.

Hardin, R. (1995) Contested community. *Society*, Vol. 32, Issue 5 (July/Aug), pp. 1–7, accessed online at http://search.epnet.com/direct.asp?an=9507106193anddb=afh, 13 February 2006.

Hargreaves, A. (1992) *Contrived Collegiality: the Micropolitics of Teacher Collaboration*. In N. Bennett, M. Crawford and C.R. Riches (eds), *Managing Change in Education: Individual and Organizational Perspectives*. London, Paul Chapman.

Hargreaves, D. (1995) School culture, school effectiveness and school improvement. *School Effectiveness and School Improvement*, Vol. 6, No. 1, pp. 23–46.

Harinck, F., De Dreu, C. and Vianen, A. (2000) The impact of conflict issues on fixed-pie perceptions, problem-solving and integrative outcomes in negotiation. *Organizational Behaviour and Human Decision Processes*, Vol. 81, No. 2, pp. 329–358.

Harris, A. (2004) Distributed leadership and school improvement: leading or misleading? *Educational Management and Administration*, Vol. 32, No. 1, pp. 11–24.

Hartle, F. and Thomas, K. (2003) *Growing Tomorrow's School Leaders – The Challenge*. Nottingham, NCSL.

Hayek. F.A. (1976) *The Mirage of Social Justice*. London, Routledge and Kegan Paul.

HEFCE (2004) *Equality and Diversity Monitoring in Higher Education Institutions: A Guide to Good Practice*. London, HEFCE.

Henze, R., Katz, A., Norte, E., Sather, S. and Walker, E. (2001) *Leading for Diversity: How School Leaders Promote Positive Interethnic Relations*. Center for Research on Education. Diversity and Excellence accessed online at http://repositories.cdlib.org/crede/edupractrpts/epr07, 12 September 2005.

Hodgkinson, C. (1996) *Administrative Philosophy: Values and Motivation in Administrative Life*. Oxford, Pergamon.

Home Office Communication Directorate (2004) *Strength in Diversity*. London, Home Office.

Hopkins, D. (1994) School improvement in an era of change. In P. Ribbins and E. Burridge (eds), *Improving Education: Promoting Quality in School*. London, Cassell.

Howard, M. and Tibballs, S. (2003) *Talking Inequality*. London, Future Foundation.

Hoyle, E. (1986) *The Politics of School Management*. London, Hodder & Stoughton.

Hurley, A.E. (1996) Challenges in cross-gender mentoring relationships: psychological intimacy, myths, rumours, innuendoes and sexual harassment. *Leadership and Organization Development Journal*, Vol. 17, No. 3, pp. 42–49.

Ian Dodds Consulting (2006) *Taking an Honest Look at your Business Culture from a Diversity Perspective*, accessed online at http://www.iandoddsconsulting.com/features.html, 31 August 2006.

Iles, P. and Kaur Hayers, P. (1997) Managing diversity in transnational project teams. A tentative model and case study. *Journal of Managerial Psychology*, Vol. 1, No. 2, pp. 95–117.

Institute of Personnel Development (1996) *Managing Diversity, an IPD Position Paper*. London, IPD.

Irby, B.J., Brown, G. and Duffy, J.A. (2001) The synergistic leadership theory. *Journal of Educational Administration*, Vol. 40, No. 4, pp. 304–322.

Jackson, J. (1993) Realistic group conflict theory: a review and evaluation of the theoretical and empirical literature. *Psychological Record*, Vol. 43, Issue 3, pp. 1–15, accessed online at http://search.epnet.com/direct.asp?an=9312270962anddb=afh, 15 April 2006.

Johnson, W. and Packer, A. (1987) *Workforce 2000: Work and Workers for the 21st Century*. Indianapolis, Hudson Institute.

Jones, C. (2006) Falling between the cracks: what diversity means for black women in higher education. *Policy Futures in Education*, Vol. 4, No. 2, pp. 145–159.

King, J.E. (2004) Dysconscious racism: ideology, identity, and the miseducation of teachers. In G. Ladson-Billings and D. Gillborn (eds), *The RoutledgeFalmer Reader in Multicultural Education*. Abingdon, RoutledgeFalmer.

Korac-Kakabadse, A. and Korac-Kakabadse, N. (1997) Best Practice in the Australian Public Service. *Journal of Managerial Psychology*, Vol. 12, No. 7, pp. 433–491.

Korac-Kakabadse, A. and Kouzmin, A. (1999) Designing for cultural diversity in an IT and globalizing milieu. *Journal of Management Development*, Vol. 18, No. 3, pp. 91–319.

Kotter, J. (1999) Making change happen. In F. Hesslebein and P. Cohen (eds), *Leader to Leader*. San Francisco, CA, Jossey–Bass.

Kram, K. (1983) Phases of the mentor relationship. *Academy of Management Journal*, Vol. 26, No. 4, pp. 608–625.

Kruger, M.L. (1996) Gender issues in school headship: quality versus power? *European Journal of Education*, Vol. 31, No. 4, pp. 447–461.

Lakomski, G. (2001) Organizational change, leadership and learning: culture as cognitive process. *The International Journal of Educational Management*, Vol. 15, No. 2, pp. 68–77.

Langlois, L. (2004) Responding ethically: complex decision–making by school district superintendents. *International Studies in Educational Administration*, Vol. 32, No. 2, pp. 78–93.

Larmore, C. (1996) *Morals of Modernity*. New York, Cambridge University Press.

Leithwood, K. and Duke, D.L. (1998) Mapping the conceptual terrain of leadership: a critical point for departure for cross-cultural studies. In P. Hallinger and K. Leithwood (eds), *Leading Schools in a Global Era: A Cultural Perspective. Peabody Journal of Education*, Vol. 73, No. 2, pp. 81–105.

Leithwood, K., Jantzi, D. and Steinbach, R. (1999) *Changing Leadership for Changing Times*. Buckingham, Open University Press.

Leonard, P. (1998) Gendering change? Management, masculinity and the dynamics of incorporating. *Gender and Education*, 10 (1), pp. 71–84.

Levin, J. (2001) *Globalizing the Community College: Strategies for Change in the Twenty First Century*. New York, Palgrave.

Lieberman, A. and Miller, L. (1999) *Teachers Transforming their World and their Work*. New York, Teachers College.

Liff, S. and Wajcman, J. (1996) 'Sameness' and 'difference' revisited: which way forward for equal opportunity initiatives? *Journal of Management Studies*, Vol. 33, No. 1, pp. 79–94.

Litvin, D.R. (1997) The discourse of diversity: from biology to management. *Discourse and Organization*, Vol. 4, No. 2, pp. 187–209.

Lopez, G.R. (2003) The (racially neutral) politics of education: a critical race theory perspective. *Educational Administration Quarterly*, Vol. 39, No. 1, pp. 68–94.

Lorbiecki, A. (2001) Changing views on diversity management: the rise of the learning perspective and the need to recognize social and political contradictions. *Management Learning*, Vol. 32, No. 3, pp. 345–361.

Lorbiecki, A. and Jack, G. (2000) Critical turns in the evolution of diversity management. *British Journal of Management*, Vol. 11, Issue 3, pp. 17–31.

Lumby, J. (2001) *Managing Further Education Colleges: Learning Enterprise*. London, Paul Chapman.

Lumby, J. (2006) Conceptualising diversity and leadership: evidence from ten cases. *Educational Management and Administration*, Vol. 34, No. 2, pp. 151–165.

Lumby, J. and Morrison, M. (2006) Partnership, conflict and gaming. *Journal of Education Policy*, Vol. 21, No. 3, pp. 323–341.

Lumby, J. and Wilson, M. (2003) Developing 14–19 education: meeting needs and improving choice. *Journal of Education Policy*, Vol. 18, No. 5, pp. 533–550.

Lumby, J., Harris, A., Morrison, M., Muijs, D., Sood, K., Glover, D., Wilson, M. with Briggs, A.R.J. and Middlewood, D. (2005) *Leadership, Development and Diversity in the Learning and Skills Sector*. London, LSDA.

Lumby, J., Muijs, D., Briggs, A., Glover, D., Harris, A., Middlewood, D., Morrison, M., Sood, K. and Wilson, M. (2004) *Leadership, Development and Diversity: The Means of Organisational Transformation?* Early soundings from the field. Paper presented to the Centre for Excellence Conference, Birmingham, 30 March 2004.

Mabokela, R.O. and Madsen, J. (2003) 'Color-blind' leadership and intergroup conflict. *Journal of School Leadership*, Vol. 13, No. 2, pp. 130–158.

Mackay, F. and Etienne, J. (2006) Black managers in further education: career hopes and hesitations. In *Educational Management, Administration and Leadership*, Vol. 34, No. 1, pp. 9–28.

Mandell, N. (1995) *Feminist Issues: Race, Class and Sexuality*. Scarborough, Ontario, Prentice-Hall.

Marshall, C. (1997) Dismantling and reconstructing policy analysis. In *Feminist Critical Policy Analysis: A Perspective from Primary and Secondary Schooling*. London, Falmer.

Maxwell, G.A., Blair, S. and McDougall, M. (2001) Edging towards managing diversity in practice. *Employee Relations*, Vol. 23, No. 5, pp. 468–482.

Maznevski, M. (1994) Understanding our differences: performance in decision-making groups with diverse members. *Human Relations*, Vol. 47, No. 5, pp. 1–16, accessed online   at http://proquest.umi.com/pqdweb?index=4anddid, 22 May 2006.

McCaffery, P. (2005) Wider management mentoring programme for women and ethnic minority managers in particular – in partnership with the public and private sector. In *Leadership Foundation Fellowships Programme*. London, 7 November.

McClellan, R. and Dominguez, R. (2006) The uneven march toward social justice: Diversity, conflict, and complexity in educational administration programs. *Journal of Educational Administration*, Vol. 44, No. 3, pp. 225–238.

McKenley, J. and Gordon, G. (2002) *Challenge Plus: The Experience of Black and Minority Ethnic School Leaders*. Nottingham, NCSL.

Milliken, Frances J. and Martins, Luis L. (1996) Searching for common threads: understanding the multiple effects of diversity in organizational groups. *Academy of Management Review,* Vol. 21, No. 2, pp. 1–32, accessed online at http:// search.epnet.com/dierct.asp?an=9605060217anddb=buh, 6 May 2004.

Mirza, H. (2006) Transcendence over diversity: black women in the academy. *Policy Futures in Education,* Vol. 4, No. 2, pp. 101–113.

Moller Okin, S. (1999) *Is Multiculturalism Bad for Women?* Princeton, NJ, Princeton University Press.

Moller Okin, S. (2002) 'Mistresses of their own destiny', group rights, gender and realistic rights of exit. *Ethics,* Vol. 112, pp. 205–230.

Monge-Najera, J.A., Rivas-Rossi, M. and Mendez-Estrada, V.H. (2001) Internet, multimedia and virtual laboratories in a 'Third World' environment. *Open Learning,* Vol. 16, No. 3, pp. 279–290.

Mor Barak, M. (2000) The inclusive workplace: an ecosystems approach to diversity management. *Social Work,* Vol. 45, No. 4, pp. 339–351.

More, Thomas (edited Logan, G. and Niller, C., trans. Adams, R.A (1994) *Utopia.* London, Phoenix.

Moreau, M.P., Osgood, J. and Halsall, A. (2005) *The Career Progression of Women Teachers in England: A Study of Barriers to Promotion and Career Development.* London, IPSE.

Morgan, G. (1986) *Images of Organization.* London, Sage.

Morris, J. (1999) Managing women: secondary school principals in Trinidad and Tobago. *Gender and Education,* Vol. 11, No. 3, pp. 343–355.

Morrison, M. and Lumby, J. (2006) *Equal Status Review: An Audit of Equal Status at XX School,* prepared for XX Education Authority and the Equality Authority of Ireland. Lincoln, University of Lincoln.

Moses, M. and Marin, P. (2006) Informing the debate on race-conscious education policy. *Educational Researcher,* Vol. 35, No. 1, pp. 3–5.

Nemetz, P. and Christensen, S. (1996) The challenge of cultural diversity: harnessing a diversity of views to understand multiculturalism. *Academy of Management Review,* Vol. 21, No. 2, pp. 434–462.

Nicholas, H. (1997) Varieties of altruism – and the common ground between them. *Social Research,* Vol. 67, No. 2, pp. 199–210.

Noddings, N. (1988) An ethic of caring and its implications for instructional arrangements. *American Journal of Education,* Vol. 96, pp. 215–230.

Norte, E. (1999) 'Structures beneath the skin': how school leaders use their power and authority to create institutional opportunities for developing positive interethnic communities. *Journal of Negro Education,* 68 (4), pp. 466–485.

North West Change Centre of Manchester Business School (2002) *Diversity – The Key to Modernization and the Bedrock of Democracy.* Manchester, Manchester Business School.

Norton, R. and Fox, R. (1997) *Change Equation: Capitalizing on Diversity for Effective Organizational Change.* Washington, DC, American Psychological Association.

Nussbaum, M. (1999a) Women and equality: the capabilities approach. *International Labour Review,* Vol. 138, No. 3, pp. 227–245.

Nussbaum, M. (1999b) *Women and Human Development: The Capabilities Approach.* Cambridge, Cambridge University Press.

Nussbaum, M. (2002) *Beyond the Social Contract: Toward Global Justice.* The Tanner Lectures on Human Values, delivered at Australian National University, Canberra, 12 and 13 November 2002 and at Clare Hall, University of Cambridge, 5 and 6 March 2003.

Oakley, A. (2002) *Gender on Planet Earth.* Cambridge, Polity Press.

Ochbuki, K. and Suzuki, M. (2003) Three dimensions of conflict issues and their effects on resolution strategies in organizational settings. *International Journal of Conflict Management*, Vol. 14, No. 1, pp. 61–73.

OECD (Organization for Economic Co-operation and Development) (2004) Gender Co-ordination at the OECD: Second Annual Report, accessed online at www.oecd.org/dataoecd/58/61/32139347.pdf, 7 May 2006.

Osler, A. (1997) *The Education and Careers of Black Teachers.* Buckingham, Open University Press.

Osler, A. (2004) Changing leadership and schools: diversity, equality and citizenship. *Race Equality Teaching*, Vol. 22, No. 3, pp. 22–28.

Osler, A. (2006) Changing leadership in contexts of diversity: visibility, invisibility and democratic ideals. *Policy Futures in Education*, Vol. 4, No. 2, pp. 128–144.

Ouston, J. (Ed.) (1993) *Women in Education Management.* Harlow, Longman.

Ozga, J. (Ed.) (1993) *Women in Educational Management.* Buckingham, Open University Press.

Patrickson, M. and Hartman, L. (2001) Human resource management in Australia: prospects for the twenty-first century. *International Journal of Manpower*, Vol. 22, No. 3, pp. 198–206.

Pearce, R. (2003) Cultural values for international schools. *International Schools Journal*, Vol. 22, No. 2, pp. 59–65.

Peters, A. (1996) The many meanings of equality and positive action in favour of women under European Community law – a conceptual analysis. *European Law Journal*, Vol. 2, No. 2, pp. 177–196.

Pitt, A. (1987) A correlation of leadership trait theory with follower traits. *Educational Administrator*, No. 29, pp. 41–48.

Powney, J., Wilson, V., Hall, S., Davidson, J., Kirk, S., Edward, S., in conjunction with Mirza, H. (2003) *Teachers' Careers: The Impact of Age, Disability, Ethnicity, Gender and Sexual Orientation*, Research Report 488. London DfES.

Prasad, P. and Mills, M. (1997) From Showcase to Shadow: Understanding Dilemmas of Managing Workplace Diversity. In P. Prasad, M. Mills, M. Elmes and A. Prasad, (eds), *Managing the Organizational Melting Pot: Dilemmas of Workplace Diversity.* London, Sage.

Quantz, R.A. and Rogers, J. (1991) Rethinking transformative leadership: toward democratic reform of schools. *Journal of Education*, Vol. 173, No. 3, pp. 1–16, accessed online at http://web22.epnet.com.uk, 6 December 2005.

Quong, T., Walker, A. and Stott, K. (1998) *Values-Based Strategic Planning*. Singapore, Simon and Schuster.

Randle, K. and Brady, N. (1997) Further education and the new managerialism. *Journal of Further and Higher Education*, Vol. 21, No. 2, pp. 229–239.

Rawls, J. (1993) *Political Liberalism*. New York: Columbia University Press.

Reay, D. (2001) The paradox of contemporary femininities in education: combining fluidity with fixity. In B. Francis and C. Skelton (eds), *Investigating Gender: Contemporary Perspective in Education*. Buckingham, Open University Press.

Reay, D. and Ball, S. (2000) Essentials of female management: women's ways of working in the education market place? *Educational Management and Administration*, Vol. 28, No. 2, pp. 145–160.

Reynolds, M. and Trehan, K. (2003) Learning from difference? *Management Learning*, Vol. 34, No. 2, pp. 163–180.

Richmon, M.J. (2004) Values in educational administration: them's fighting words! *International Journal of Leadership in Education*, Oct–Dec 2004, Vol. 7, Issue 4, pp. 339–356.

Roberts, B. (2003) What should international education be? From emergent theory to practice. *International Schools Journal*, Vol. 22, No. 2, pp. 69–79.

Roche, K. (1999) Moral and ethical dilemmas in Catholic school settings. In P. Begley (ed.), *Values and Educational Leadership*. Albany, NY, State University of New York Press.

Ross-Smith, A. and Kornberger, M. (2004) Gendered rationality? A genealogical exploration of the philosophical and sociological conceptions of rationality, masculinity and organization. *Gender, Work and Organization*, Vol. 11, No. 3, pp. 280–305.

Ruijs, A. (1993) *Women Managers in Education – A Worldwide Progress Report*. Bristol, The Staff College, Coombe Lodge Report.

Rusch, E. (2004) Gender and race in leadership preparation: a constrained discourse. *Educational Administration Quarterly*, Vol. 40, No. 1, pp. 16–48.

Russell, M. (2003) Leadership and followership as a relational process. *Educational Management and Administration*, Vol. 31, No. 2, pp. 145–157.

Sanglin-Grant, S. and Schneider, R. (2000) *Moving On Up? Racial Equality and the Corporate Agenda*. London, Runnymede Trust.

Sapolsky, R. (2002) Cheaters and chumps. *Natural History*, Vol. 111, No. 5, pp. 1–7, accessed online at http://weblinks2.epnet.com/citation.asp?, 23 May 2006.

Schagen, S., Johnson, F. and Simkin, C. (1996) *Sixth Form Options – Post-compulsory Education in Maintained Schools*. Slough, NFER.

Schein, V.E. (1994) Managerial sex typing: a persistent and pervasive barrier to women's opportunities. In M. Davidson and R. Burke (eds), *Women in Management: Current Research Issues*. London, Paul Chapman.

Schminke, M., Ambrose, M.L. and Neubaum, D.O. (2005) The effect of leader moral development on ethical climate and employee attitudes. *Organizational Behavior and Human Decision Processes*, Vol. 97, No. 2, pp. 135–151.

Schmuck, P. (1996) Women's place in educational administration: past, present and future. In K. Leithwood, J. Chapman, D. Corson, P. Hallinger and A. Hart (eds), *International Handbook of Educational Leadership and Administration*. Boston, MA, Kluwer Academic.

Sen, A. (1984) *Resources, Values and Development*. Cambridge, MA, Harvard University Press.

Sergiovanni, T. (1993) *Organisations or Communities: Changing the Metaphor Changes the Theory*. AERA Invited Address, Division A, Atlanta, GA.

Shah, S. (2006a) Leading multiethnic schools: a new understanding of Muslim youth identity. *Educational Management Administration and Leadership*, Vol. 34, No. 2, pp. 215–237.

Shah, S. (2006b) Educational leadership: an Islamic perspective. *British Educational Research Journal*, Vol. 32, No. 3, pp. 363–386.

Shain, F. (1999) *Managing to Lead: Women Managers in the Further Education Sector*. Paper presented at the BERA annual conference, University of Sussex at Brighton, 2–5 September 1999.

Shakeshaft, C. (1989) *Women in Educational Administration*. Newbury Park, CA, Sage.

Sherif, M. and Sherif, C. (1953) *Groups in Harmony and Tension: An Integration of Studies on Intergroup Relations*. New York, Harper.

Shukra, K., Back, L., Keith, M., Khan, A. and Solomos, J. (2004) Race, social cohesion and the changing politics of citizenship. *London Review of Education*, Vol. 2, No. 3, pp. 187–195.

Simkins, T. (2000) Education reform and managerialism: comparing the experience of schools and colleges. *Journal of Education Policy*, Vol. 15, No. 3, pp. 317–332.

Simkins, T. and Lumby, J. (2002) Cultural transformation in further education? Mapping the debate. *Research in Post-Compulsory Education*, Vol. 7, No. 1, pp. 9–25.

Simons, T. and Pelled, L.H. (1999) Understanding executive diversity: more than meets the eye. *Human Resource Planning*, Vol. 22, Issue 2, pp. 49–51.

Sinclair, A. (2000) Women within diversity: risks and possibilities. *Women in Management Review*, Vol. 15, No. 5/6, pp. 237–245.

Sinclair, A. (2004) Journey around leadership. *Discourse*, Vol. 25, No. 1, pp. 7–19.

Singh, V. (2002) *Managing Diversity for Strategic Advantage*. London, Council for Excellence in Management and Leadership.

Smith, M.B. Jnr (1997) Are traditional management tools sufficient for diverse teams? *Team Performance Management*, Vol. 3, No. 1, pp. 3–11.

Smithers, R. (2005) London schools still struggling three years after Blair initiative. The *Guardian*, (London), p. 12.

Smithson, J. and Stokoe, E. (2005) Discourses of work–life balance: negotiating 'genderblind' terms in organizations. *Gender, Work and Organization*, Vol. 12, No. 2, pp. 147–168.

Smulyan, L. (2000) *Balancing Acts: Women Principals at Work*. Albany, NY, New York State University.

Southworth, G. (2002) Instructional leadership in schools: reflections and empirical evidence. *School Leadership and Management*, Vol. 22, No. 1, pp. 73–92.

Spillane, J., Halverson, R. and Diamond, J. (2004) Towards a theory of leadership practice: a distributed perspective. *Journal of Curriculum Studies*, Vol. 36, No. 1, pp. 3–34.

Stier, J. (2006) Internationalisation, intercultural communication and intercultural competence. *Journal of Intercultural Communication*, Issue 11, pp. 1–12. accessed online at www.immi.se/intercultural/, 14 July 2006.

Stone, D. and Colella, A. (1996) A model of factors affecting the treatment of disabled individuals in organizations. *Academy of Management Review*, Vol. 12, No. 2, pp. 352–401.

Stott, C. and Lawson, L. (1997) *Women at the Top in Further Education*. London, FEDA.

Sturges, J. (1999) What it means to succeed: personal conceptions of career success held by male and female managers at different ages. *British Journal of Management*, Vol. 10, No. 3, pp. 239–252.

Thomas, D. and Ely, R. (1996) Making differences matter: a new paradigm for managing diversity. *Harvard Business Review*, Vol. 74, No. 5, pp. 79–90.

Trompenaars, F. and Hampden-Turner, C. (1997) *Riding the Waves of Culture: Understanding Cultural Diversity in Business*, 2nd edn. London, Nicholas Brealey.

Thrupp, M. and Willmott, R. (2003) *Educational Management in Managerialist Times: Beyond the Textual Apologists*. Maidenhead, Open University Press.

Tippeconnic, J. (2006) Identity based and reputational leadership: an American Indian approach to leadership. *Journal of Research in Leader Education*, accessed online at www.ucea.org/JRLE/pdf/vol1/issue1/Tippeconnic.pdf, 22 May 2006.

Tollefson, K.D. (1995) Potlatching and political organizations among the Northwest Coast Indians. Ethnology, Vol. 34, Issue No. 1, pp. 53–74, accessed online at http://search.epnet.com/direct.asp?an=9505023827anddb=afh, 18 August 2004.

Valverde, L.A. (2006) Needed: leadership for liberation. A global portrait painted in shades of brown. *Journal of Leader Education*, Vol. 1, No. 1, pp. 1–5, accessed online at www.ucea.org/JRLE/pdf/vol1/issue1/Valverde.pdf, 18 May 2006.

Vogel-Polsky, E. (1985) Positive action programmes for women. *International Labour Review*, Vol. 124, No. 3, pp. 253–265.

Walker, A. (2006) Leader development across cultures. *Journal of Research in Leader Education,* accessed online at www.ucea.org/JRLE/pdf/vol1/issue1/Walker.pdf, 22 May 2006.

Walker, A. and Walker, J. (1998) Challenging the boundaries of sameness: leadership through valuing difference. *Journal of Educational Administration*, Vol. 36, No. 1, pp. 8–28.

Wallace, M. and Hall, V. (1994) *Inside the SMT*. London, Paul Chapman.

Walther, B., Schwer, J. and Wolter, S. (2005) Shall I train your apprentice: an empirical investigation of outsourcing of apprenticeship training in Switzerland. *Education + Training*, Vol. 47, No. 4–5, pp. 251–269.

Weber, M. (trans. Henderson, A.M. and Parsons, T.) (1947) *The Theory of Social and Economic Organization*. New York, Free Press.

Weiss, A. (1999) *The Glass Ceiling: A Look at Women in the Workforce*. Brookfield, CT, Twenty-First Century Books.

Wentling, R.M. and Palma-Rivas, N. (2000) Current status of diversity initiatives in selected multinational corporations. *Human Resource Development Quarterly*, Vol. 11, No. 1, pp. 35–60.

Wikipedia (2006) Diversity. http://en.wikipedia.org/wiki/Diversity, accessed 17 May 2006.

Wilde, O. (2004) *The Soul of Man Under Socialism*. Whitefish, MT, Kessinger.

Willie, C.V. (1987) *Black and White Families: A Study in Complementarity*. New York, General Hall.

Wilson, E. and Iles, P. (1999) Managing diversity – an employment and service delivery challenge. *The International Journal of Public Sector Management*, Vol. 12, No. 1, pp. 27–48.

Woods, P. (2004) Democratic leadership: drawing distinctions with distributed leadership. *International Journal of Leadership in Education*, Vol. 7, No. 1, pp. 3–26.

Woods, G. and Woods, P. (2005) At the hard edge of change: views from secondary head teachers on a public–private partnership. *Journal of Education Policy*, Vol. 20, No. 1, p. 23–38.

Wright Mills, C. (1959) *The Sociological Imagination*. Oxford, Oxford University Press.

Yeatman, A. (1990) Bureaucrats, technocrats, femocrats: essays on the contemporary Australian State. Sydney, Allen and Unwin.

You-Ta, C., Church R. and Zikic, J. (2004) Organizational culture, group diversity and intra-group conflict. *Team Performance Management*, Vol. 10, No. 1, pp. 26–34.

Young, M. and Mountford, (2006) Infusing gender and diversity issues into educational leadership programs. *Journal of Educational Administration*, Vol. 44, No. 3, pp. 264–277.

Young, S.P. (2002) Illusions of difference? Larmore's political liberalism. *An Internet Journal of Philosophy*, Vol. 6, pp. 151–161, accessed at www.ul.ie/~philos/vol6/larmore.html, 31 August 2006.

Statutes and Regulations

All UK legislation is published by Her Majesty's Stationery Office (HMSO) and is Crown Copyright. Legislation dating from 1987 can be printed out or read online from the website of the Office of Public Sector Information at www.opsi.gov.uk

Children Act 2004
  www.opsi.gov.uk/acts/acts2004/20040031.htm
  London, HMSO, ISBN 0 10543104 4
Employment Equality (Religion or Belief) Regulations 2003
  www.opsi.gov.uk/si/si2003/20031660.htm
  London, HMSO, ISBN 0 11046676 4
Employment Equality (Sexual Orientation) Regulations 2003
  www.opsi.gov.uk/SI/si2003/20031661.htm
  London, HMSO, ISBN 0 11046677 2
Employment Act 2002
  www.opsi.gov.uk/acts/acts2002/20020022.htm
  London, HMSO, ISBN 1 10542202 9
Flexible Working (Eligibility, Complaints, Remedies) Regulations 2002
  www.opsi.gov.uk/si/si2002/20023236.htm
  London, HMSO, ISBN 0 11044463 9
Race Relations (Amendment) Act 2000
  www.opsi.gov.uk/acts/acts2000/20000034.htm
  London, HMSO, ISBN 0 10543400 0
Sex Discrimination (Gender Reassignment) Regulations 1999
  www.opsi.gov.uk/si/si1999/19991102.htm
  London, HMSO, ISBN 0 11082501
Disability Discrimination Act 1995
  www.opsi.gov.uk/acts/acts1995/1995050.htm
  London, HSMO, ISBN 0 10545095 2
Disabled Persons (Services, Consultation and Representation) Act 1986
  London, HMSO, ISBN 0 10543386 1
Sex Discrimination Act 1986
  London, HMSO
Race Relations Act 1976
  London, HMSO, ISBN 0 10547476 2

Sex Discrimination Act 1975
  London, HMSO, ISBN 0 10546575 5
Equal Pay Act 1970
  London, HMSO.
Disabled Persons Act 1958
  London, HMSO
Disabled Persons Act 1944
  London, HMSO

Author index